CHEAP ROOMS AND RESTLESS HEARTS

CHEAP ROOMS AND RESTLESS HEARTS:

A Study of Formula in the Urban Tales of William Sydney Porter

Karen Charmaine Blansfield

Bowling Green State University Popular Press
Bowling Green, Ohio 43403

Cover design by Gary Dumm

This book is dedicated to my mother and father, who above all believed in me.

CONTENTS

Acknowledgements

I would like to thank several people who helped to make this book possible.

The curators of the O. Henry Collection in the Greensboro Public Library were most courteous and cooperative in granting me access to the letters and documents housed there, and I appreciate their assistance.

I would also like to thank William Bloodworth, Professor of American literature and chairman of the English Department at East Carolina University, whose friendship and counsel I have always valued. His guidance and cheerful support enabled me to begin this manuscript in the first place, and his sound judgments have contributed greatly to the book's growth.

I am especially grateful to Dr. Douglas McMillan, also of East Carolina University, for generously taking time from his own busy schedule to read and re-read portions of the manuscript and to shuttle chapters back and forth across the country. His valuable suggestions were crucial in shaping the final manuscript, and his warm letters of encouragement bolstered me during those periods of drudgery and exasperation.

Finally, I want to extend a personal note of appreciation to Robert Zepernick for his resilience and good humor while this manuscript was being prepared. Most of all, I thank him for his affection, emotional support, and unwavering friendship which sustained me and pulled me through the dark time.

Introduction

He has been called the master of the unexpected ending, the virtuoso of the short story, the greatest of modern American writers. He has been labeled the American Gogol, de Maupassant, Boccaccio, and Rabelais, compared to Shakespeare, Dickens, and Villon. Critics have dubbed him a philosopher, a literary Haroun Al Raschid, the Homer of the Tenderloin, the Apostle of the Picaresque. He called himself O. Henry.

Admirers have praised him as a designer of stories, an extraordinarily clever literary artist, the most representative American short story writer of the turn of the century. Detractors have condemned him as theatric, stagy, snappy, and ultra-modern, as flippant and insincere, a literary harlequin choked with smokeroom smartness. His stories, to some, are like beautiful crystals that elicit gasps, masterpieces of intricate plot manufacture; to others, they smell of the footlights, they turn on a juggler's trick, they helped to cheapen the short story as a literary form.

Such are the extremes of opinion which attend the work of William Sydney Porter, the literary phenomenon of the twentieth century's first decade known to his delighted reading public as O. Henry. His work is marked by several distinguishing characteristics: mechanical, carefully structured plots, two-dimensional character types, a flavorful if often clever and playful writing style, and the well-known ironic ending which has come to be called the O. Henry twist. His calculated weaving together of these elements—with the snappy clincher as the central focus—has led to this extreme diversity of opinion about his validity as an artist, a judgment which naturally depends upon whether one sees Porter's method as brilliant mastery of technique or as clever but artificial manipulation that violates vital artistic principle.

1

Regardless of how they are judged, these qualities are intrinsic to Porter's stories, and they form the basis of his popularity, for their simplicity and cleverness are the ingredients of popular entertainment. Porter's stories do not demand much intellectual exercise on the reader's part, but they are sophisticated enough to satisfy intelligence; they are exciting and even dramatic, yet not disturbing. Furthermore, Porter's repeated use of these elements establishes a bond of familiarity for the reader. A variety of plot patterns, a gallery of character types, a folksy, confidential manner and a stock file of narrative elements and canny endings all combine to create a world of predictability and thus security.

Although Porter's stories are set in various places—Texas, Central America, and Louisiana being major locales—it is the New York stories which are the most renowned and the most popular, and it was the New York stories which launched his fame and his meteoric career. For it was in New York that Porter, stumbling from the dark prison of his past, was transfigured into the mysterious and memorable figure known as O. Henry. The city sheltered him, comforted him; he in turn endowed it with a fresh curiosity and wonder, taking it unto himself:

> He owned the city, its people were his subjects [sic]. He went into their midst, turning upon them the shrewd microscope of his gleaming understanding. Sham, paltry deceit, flimsy pose, were blown away as veils before a determined wind. The souls stood forth, naked and pathetic. The wizard had his way.[1]

Prior to 1902, when he moved to New York, Porter, although he had already published many short stories, was virtually unknown. But with his tales romanticizing the city that he christened "Little Bagdad on the Subway"—appearing in popular magazines like *Everybody's* and *McClure's* and in the Sunday supplements of the *New York World*—he became a revered and sought-after author from then until his death in 1910. Out of the 272 stories he wrote, nearly one hundred—over a third of the total output—deal with New York, and today it is the New York stories for which he is best remembered.

The New York setting of these stories is familiar and authentic for the most part, with Porter identifying specific places by name and accurately describing areas such as Madison Square, Central

Park, and Broadway. But under the spell of O. Henry, these become places of intrigue and romance. He is an Aladdin: he rubs the magic lamp of his imagination and New York becomes a city transformed:

It is no longer the roaring, surging metropolis that we thought we knew, with its clattering elevated [trains], its unending crowds, and on every side the repellent selfishness of the rich, the grim struggle of the poor, and the listless despair of the outcast. It has become, as O. Henry loves to call it, Bagdad upon the Subway. The glare has gone. There is a soft light suffusing the city. Its corner drugstores turn to enchanted bazaars. From the open doors of its restaurants and palm rooms, there issues such a melody of softened music that we feel we have but to cross the threshold and there is Bagdad waiting for us beyond.[2]

Night, especially, was the magical hour for him. "When the million lights flashed and throngs of men and women crowded the thorough-fares in long, undulating lines like moving, black snakes, Bill Porter came into his own."[3]

Against this background, his stories chronicle the lives of the common people who comprise the "four million" of New York. Porter found "a thousand wonder tales to be told of the lives of the derelicts sleeping on the benches of Madison Square, of the humble dwellers in Harlem flats, and of the half-educated girls behind the glove counters in the big department stores."[4] These characters—the shopgirls, the tramps, and the flat-dwellers, the wealthy aristocrats and the poverty-ridden workers—appear consistently in his urban tales, becoming easily recognizable by the specific characteristics they possess as a group and by the conventional images they embody.

The plots of the stories, too, become recognizable by virtue of repetition. Porter, while employing a number of variations, draws upon a limited group of plot patterns for these stories, patterns which also embrace some themes familiar to readers. The basic elements of these character and plot types are common to other Porter stories as well, but in the urban short stories they are presented distinctively in terms of cultural surroundings. The characters are born of the city and shaped by it; the plots are constructed on actions and events unique to the city. It's interesting to note, though, that Porter himself might disagree with this assessment, judging by what he once said in an interview:

People say I know New York well. Just change Twenty-third Street in one of my New York stories to Main Street, rub out the Flatiron Building and put in the Town Hall, and the story will fit just as truly in any up-state town. At least, I hope this can be said of my stories. So long as a story is true to human nature all you need do is change the local color to make it fit any town, North, East, South or West. If you have the right kind of an eye—the kind that can disregard high hats, cutaway coats and trolley cars—you can see all the characters in the 'Arabian Nights' parading up and down Broadway at mid-day.[5]

Because of this juxtaposition of general types and patterns with specific cultural settings and themes, and because of the dominant element of repetition, Porter's narrative art assumes a formulaic nature. A close examination of the major plot patterns employed as narrative structure, along with the character types most frequently portrayed, types which are both conventional and universal, reveals the formulaic elements in these urban short stories.

The concept of formula, which will be discussed more fully in Chapter Two, is fundamental to the oldest types of literature known: the oral forms and their derivatives. Folktales, fables, fairy stories, folk ballads are all built upon patterns that become familiar through repetition, with character types who also become easily recognizable by their continual reappearance. Long after primary archetypal tales and songs had receded into the dim mists of the past, literature continued to draw upon those well-established patterns of plot and character, and though it has become more sophisticated and diverse, a broad span of literature is still built upon the framework of formula.

Archetypal patterns—in plot, character, image, event, and other forms—have provided a constant, unchanging basis for the evolution of human literature, creating a rhythm and a familiarity that links the most modern literature with the most ancient. "The latest incarnation of Oedipus, the continued romance of Beauty and the Beast, stand this afternoon on the corner of Forty-second Street and Fifth Avenue, waiting for the traffic light to change."[6]

There is a comfort, a security in listening to these old tales and songs over and over, in whatever guise they appear, especially for children but also for adults. "In that well-known and controlled landscape of the imagination, the tensions, ambiguities, and frustrations of ordinary experience are painted over by magic pigments of adventure, romance and mystery. The world for a time takes on the shape of our heart's desire."[7]

Too often, the more modern versions of such literature have been criticized as vapid and insignificant, written off as "escapist stuff" designed merely to entertain, not to enlighten. This is, of course, a broad generalization and an oversimplification. Naturally enough, formula material in its various guises—magazines and book fiction, radio and television drama, music, art, cartoons, and so forth—has always been quite appealing. "Popular taste has always demanded the recognizable object in a painting, the melody that can be hummed, the order of words that is easy to follow."[8] Such widespread popularity in itself makes these literary forms "artistic and cultural phenomena of tremendous importance," although because of their "escapist" tendencies, they have "been largely ignored by literary scholars and historians or left to the mercy of sociologists, psychologists, and analysts of mass culture," groups which have "largely treated them as ideological rationalization, psychological stratagems, or opiates for the masses."[9]

The commercial motive frequently underlying the creation and production of formulaic literature has been another point of suspicion, although this criticism is founded on the assumption that something produced for money is automatically second-rate, whereas masterpieces spring solely from an artist's creative impulse. Though there may be some validity to these corollaries, the danger of generalizing is obvious. Shakespeare, for instance, who was the most popular playwright of his time, surely aimed for a wide audience and sought literary fame. His masterpieces are based on familiar stories, figures, and events, and are cast in language designed to be appreciated by underlings as well as nobility. And an unknown writer named Herman Melville once wrote to his publisher, "The book is certainly calculated for popular reading, or for none at all," referring to *Typee*.[10]

Similarly, the formula artist himself has been decried as an artificer, a manipulator who lacks vision and talent, a manufacturer of cultural products on demand. Again, this is a sweeping accusation that lacks discrimination, for even the basest formula writing demands some skills and talents, whose execution can range from mere competence to flourishing brilliance.

As a popular artist, William Sydney Porter certainly catered to the whims of public taste and leaned heavily upon formula to churn out his material. One need only read a dozen or so of his tales at one sitting to discover how easy it becomes to predict the endings. But of course such predictability is part of his—and any popular artist's—charm.

In this study, the examination of the formulaic patterns which Porter evolved will proceed through five stages. First of all, it must be remembered that Porter was influenced by the age in which he lived and by the public he sought to please, as well as by the events of his own life. Chapter One of this study offers a brief biography of Porter, emphasizing those developments most relevant to his career as a writer and to the type of literature he would produce; it also looks at the social and cultural climate in America at the turn of the century to suggest how time and place helped to shape Porter's literary formulas and to elevate him to his position as popular artist.

This role as popular artist, an identity which is further examined in Chapter Two, is also important to an understanding of Porter's formulaic art. As a genre, popular art is defined by certain characteristics, including the use of formula. The chapter examines how Porter and his art fit into this genre and how his particular treatment of formula helps to define his work both internally—within his own body of work—and externally—within the framework of popular literature in general. It also defines and discusses the concepts of literary formula and their applications to Porter's work, as well as outlining the plot patterns and character types to be treated in the central portion of the study.

A reading of several of Porter's short stories easily reveals the recurrence of plot structures, and Chapter Three examines the four predominant internal patterns discernible in these urban tales: the cross pattern—further subdivided into cross-purposes, crossed paths, and cross-identity—the habit pattern, the triangle pattern, and the quest pattern. In addition, the chapter points out the conventional and sometimes archetypal patterns which these stories imitate.

In Chapter Four, a similar examination is made of Porter's characters, who by their recurrence can be classified into six major types: the shopgirl, the habitual character, the lover, the aristocrat, the plebeian, and the tramp, types which are defined by specific elements. They are shown to be conventional in their makeup and behavior and also to be sketchy cultural embodiments of more universal or archetypal models.

Finally, the Conclusion evaluates Porter's position in and contributions to American popular literature, with a final discussion of his particular and distinctive style, his connection to the tradition of formulaic literature, and his ultimate artistic achievement.

Chapter One
The Life and Times of William Sydney Porter

New York City at the turn of the century was a restless, exciting place poised on the threshold of change, no longer a town yet still not the thundering metropolis it was soon to become. A provincial charm and languid romance lingered in its streets and parks, even as the rumble of urban industrialization grew louder and the bright glow of opportunity paled into the cold light of despair. This New York was a paradox, a poison and an elixir, a city rich with both promise and disillusionment, the city of Jacob Riis and John Rockefeller, where ragged workers mingled silently with gay-spirited *nouveaux riche*. At the close of the 1800s, with business, technology, and mass immigration swelling, New York was a city coming of age, relinquishing its hold on the past as it sallied forth into the new century.

Into this bewildering metropolis Porter emerged in 1902, himself a man of paradox, private and reclusive, bearing secrets as dark and hidden as the city's, yet keen and curious to peer into the lives of others and to probe their secrets. Safe among these anonymous crowds, Porter too would relinquish his hold on the past and issue forth into a new life. In the city's relentless machinery, the same machinery which was transforming human lives into mechanical ones or shabby lives into glorious ones, the tainted identity of William Sydney Porter would be transmuted into the solitary, elusive, legendary figure of O. Henry.

Who he really was and where he had come from remained a mystery during Porter's lifetime. He was surely *of* New York, but as Van Wyck Brooks noted, he "was the typical New Yorker of the popular saying, the man who has come from somewhere else. . . ."[1] Not until after his death was the O. Henry of New York unveiled as the William Sydney Porter of Ohio and Central America, vagabond fugitive and destitute prisoner. From his beginnings in North Carolina just five hundred miles to the south, he had landed in New York at the end of a long and circuitous route through Texas, Central America, South America, the Ohio penitentiary, and Pittsburgh. His own life reads like a romantic adventure tale studded with character types all played by Porter himself: Southern gentleman, ranch hand and pseudo-cowboy, husband, father, bank teller and businessman, victim of circumstance and wanted criminal, plantation dandy, prodigal son, prisoner, loner. All fiction is tame, he once said, "compared with the romance of my own life."[2] His childhood influences and memories, his cache of adventures and observations, and the humiliating stigma of prison life, would all shape his vision of and response to the city in which he finally dwelled. In fact, Porter's life and literary career in New York were in many ways the necessary culmination of all that had come before.

A Southerner by descent, Porter spent twenty-two years—nearly half his life—in his native Greensboro, North Carolina, where he was born in 1862. Greensboro was still a somnolent little Southern town[3] then, even though these two decades were rooted in the Civil War and Reconstruction. While Porter's childhood and adolescence there were uneventful, the region itself, with its languid, easy pace and sweet Southern romance, would nurture and shape the soul and spirit of the youthful Porter and the future O. Henry.

Even then he was a quiet, reticent sort, a sensitive young man with a penchant for serenading with his violin and for roaming the outdoors, "a dreamer, a thinker, and a constant reader."[4] That Lane's *Thousand and One Arabian Nights* and Burton's *Anatomy of Melancholy* were his favorite classics is by now one of the most well-known details about him, as is the fact that he devoured books. "I did more reading between my thirteenth and nineteenth years than I have done in all the years since," he commented in an interview not long before his death.[5]

His reputation as a humorist, an artist, a tale-teller, and a sharp observer of life and human nature was flourishing even then. When he went out tramping and traveling with his friends, he was always absorbed by the character of every small town, and with keen interest he "recalled vividly characteristics of the communities and their inhabitants which had been unnoticed by the other boys."[6]

In the classroom and the informal gatherings conducted by his Aunt Lina, the reading of good literature and the telling of tales were important elements, and Porter was quick to gain preeminence as a spinner of yarns. In his uncle's drug store, too, where young Porter worked—gaining pharmaceutical experience that would also prove crucial later in his life—he watched and listened closely to the local folk who gathered there to pass the time and swap tales round the old wood stove, further enriching the imagination of this future Scheherezade. "Those patrons and loungers were a curious study in character types of the old South,"[7] and Porter's sketches of them, harbingers of O. Henry, seized upon some central trait, some peculiar characteristic "to interpret and reveal the character as a whole";[8] they earned him a local fame (and perhaps some local resentment as well from those who were caricatured unflatteringly). "When somebody he did not know asked for credit or paid a bill during Clark Porter's [his uncle's] absence, Will drew a sketch of him, so vividly that his uncle never failed to recognize the person."[9]

Even more telling were the group drawings Porter made, portraits which "came close to social history in depicting the life of the community,"[10] and which in his biographer's analysis foreshadowed the future storyteller:

There is the same selection of a central theme, the same saturation with a controlling idea, the same careful choice of contributory details, the same rejection of non-essentials, and the same ability to fuse both theme and details into a single totality of effect.[11]

Porter left Greensboro in March of 1882, and though he was to return only a few times more during his lifetime—and then but briefly—he retained his Southern identity and mannerisms throughout his life. In a letter written a few years before his death, he expressed a sentimental nostalgia for the somnolent old home town, saying,

I take my pen in hand to say that I am from the South and have been a stranger in New York for four years.

**   **   **

> I was born and raised in 'No'th Ca'lina' and...I was thinking lately (since the April moon commenced to shine) how I'd like to be down South, where I could happen over to Miss Ethel's or Miss Sallie's and sit on the porch—not a chair—on the edge of the porch, and lay my straw hat on the steps and lay my head back against the honeysuckle on the post—and just talk.[12]

This might be construed as rather false sentiment, for in fact Porter *did* return to North Carolina, in the fall of 1909, the year before he died. But it offered "too much scenery and fresh air,"[13] and by the following March he was back in New York, which had by then become an inseparable part of him. "I could look at these mountains a hundred years and never get an idea," he said to his wife in Asheville, "but just one block downtown and I catch a sentence, see something in a face—and I've got my story."[14]

Such contrariety pervades Porter's life as well as the characters and plot structures of his stories. This duplicity, which marks both the man and the artist, is a central force shaping Porter's life and, in turn, his art. In fact, as will be noted later, Porter's need to bridge the gaps in a life crippled by fate and circumstance is often projected onto the characters he creates.

At the time of his death, Porter had even been planning a work based on the Southern identity and Southern types, a work which had already been contracted for serialization by an editor of *Collier's Weekly*. Porter had wished to contrast the "professional" and "decadent" Southerners, "the useless, shiftless, lazy individual who still lives with the Civil War and blames it for his unfortunate condition in life," and the hustling "red-headed producer of results who is so busy making good that he has even forgotten that there was such a thing as the Spanish-American War."[15] But of course the story, with its author's characteristic contrariness, was never written.

Ill health and small-town ennui prompted Porter's exodus from Greensboro to Texas, although letters back to North Carolina would reflect mixed feelings of homesickness tempered by a resolve not to return until successful. The years Porter spent in Texas—from 1882 until early 1898, excluding the months from July 1896 through February 1897—formed a crucial chapter in his life, for they not only encompassed the major rites of passage, they also saw radical shifts in Porter's fortunes, from the happiest days of his life to the darkest hours he would ever know. This span of years heralded significant events for the young Porter: his marriage, the birth of his daughter, the death of his ill-fated young wife, and most critical of all, the passage from free man to fugitive to prisoner, initiating the long, painful journey which would ultimately transform Porter into O. Henry.

He spent his Texas years first on a ranch, then in Austin—the longest and most significant period—and finally in Houston, where he lived for the last few months of his Texas period, before the tangled web of circumstance finally ensnared him. During all this time, Porter gathered vital experiences and acquired knowledge from which he would draw during his later literary career.

For a romantic dreamer like Porter, life on a sheep ranch outside Cotulla, Texas, promised adventure of legendary proportions. Although the young man still remained more an observer of life than a participant, he gained plenty of first-hand experience about the rhythms and routines of ranch life, of character types like cowboys, desperadoes, rangers, and rustlers, and of the vast, lonesome landscape, the desert and plains and chaparrals that would grace his later stories. He learned about war between ranchmen and cattle thieves; he learned about "the real desperado...the outlaw, the ranger, the Mexican sheepherder, and the cowboy troubadour—all of whom were to figure in his stories of the Southwest."[16]

This new kind of life filled Porter's mind "with that rich variety of types and adventures which later was translated into his stories." Here he drew "the originals of his western characters and western scenes. He looked on at the more picturesque life about him rather than shared in it; though through his warm sympathy and his vivid imagination he entered into its spirit as completely as anyone who had fully lived its varied parts."[17]

Even in his correspondence, he reveals a natural and increasingly adept reaction to characters as types, delineating them in the same focused style as his earlier sketches and his later stories. In his last letter to North Carolina from the ranch, for example, he wrote:

Spring has opened and the earth is clothed in verdure new. The cowboy has doffed his winter apparel and now appeareth in his summer costume of a blue flannel shirt and spurs. An occasional norther still swoops down upon him, but he buckles on an extra six shirts and defies the cold.[18]

In other ways the future O. Henry was also taking shape. The young Porter studied languages: some French and German but mainly Mexican-Spanish, which he was able to absorb because of its widespread use around him. He read avidly—fiction, history, biography, science, magazines, poetry (he loved Tennyson)—and especially the dictionary, which he perused voraciously; it was during this time "that he laid the foundation of the fastidious and accurate vocabulary that was later to delight readers and astound the critics."[19]

When he moved to Austin in the spring of 1884, this pattern of learning and astute observation continued. His life in the city "was marked by the same sort of quick and wide-reaching reaction to his environment that had already become characteristic and that was to culminate during his eight years in New York. . . . His friends in Austin say that no one ever touched the city at so many points or knew its social strata as familiarly as O. Henry."[20]

Porter worked for a short time as a drug clerk, then as a bookkeeper, then for a longer period as draftsman in a Land Office—a position he lost when his employer was defeated in an election, followed by the fateful stint at the First National Bank of Austin, which he resigned in December of 1894, convinced that business was not his line of work.

In a romantic escapade evocative of an O. Henry story, Porter eloped with Athol Estes in July, 1887, and about two years later a daughter Margaret, his only child, was born. His marriage and settled home life was, according to some biographers, a source of great contentment for Porter; others contend that it produced tensions and unhappiness, Athol being a spoiled young woman because of her fragile health. Considering Porter's romantic nature combined with his innate restlessness and curiosity, the situation was probably a combination of both. Whatever his sentiments, it was no doubt the dual demands of home life and a dull bank routine, along with growing literary impulses, that propelled Porter to undertake his editorial endeavor with the *Rolling Stone* as one creative outlet. Rather ironically, this brief literary venture may have been what led to the dismal chain of events which would in turn land Porter on the path to literary fame. For according to one theory, the funds Porter allegedly embezzled from the First National Bank were "borrowed" to help sustain the struggling newspaper.

At any rate, Porter and his partner James Crane—later replaced by Dixie Daniels—produced the ten-page humorous weekly themselves, a pastiche of articles, satire, sketches, political burlesque, cartoons, and a rather ingenious, stinging parody of small town newspapers dubbed "The Plunkville Patriot."

On the whole, Porter's *Rolling Stone* ranged in quality from mundane to quite respectable, and its contents typify the style and attitude that define the author's later work. One critic, in fact, judges this editorial experience to have been the most significant phase in "the development of Will Porter into O. Henry."[21] The material is marked by the same sort of humor that would later distinguish Porter's stories; a keen eye for character detail suggests his future method "as a photographic portrayer of odd types of humanity";[22] the sharply satirical commentary shows plainly his strong sympathy "with the downtrodden that was later to be a characteristic of O. Henry's short stories";[23] and his colorful accounts of city life are drawn from the same vagrant wanderings that mark his New York days:

Like the Calif Haroun al Raschid, but without his power of relieving distress or punishing wickedness, I often stroll about Austin studying nature and reading many pages in the great book of Man.[24]

But of course at that time, Porter was still an unknown, and none of these now-significant qualities was sufficient to keep the publication rolling; according to Dixie Daniels, the *Rolling Stone* ultimately succumbed by alienating local ethnic and political groups. The first issue had appeared on April 28, 1894, the last on April 27, 1895. "It rolled for about a year and then showed unmistakable signs of getting mossy," Porter said later. "Moss and I never were friends, and so I said good-bye to *The Rolling Stone*."[25]

In the meantime, though, Porter had quit his position as teller at the First National Bank, a move which was probably unwise, perhaps critical, and surely suspicious, for a discrepancy was soon discovered in his accounts, so that his resignation implied guilt.

Whether Porter was guilty or innocent of absconding with bank funds is a mystery that will remain forever unsolved. Strong arguments have been made on both sides, but ultimately the judgment, like a jury's, must be subjective, since no conclusive facts exist, even though some evidence is strongly persuasive. That the bank was notoriously sloppy in its record-keeping is undisputed: officers were known to help themselves to cash freely, without noting withdrawals, and as Porter's biographer grimly points out, "The affairs of the bank were managed so loosely that Porter's predecessor was driven to retirement, his successor to attempted suicide."[26]

That Porter's newspaper was floundering at the time is also clear, as is the fact that he borrowed money from his father-in-law in the struggle to keep it afloat. Then of course, Porter was a dreamer still, sneaking moments behind his teller's cage to sketch his caricatures, but he had also been regarded in his previous bookkeeping job as accurate and extremely diligent. Later, in his New York years, Porter was undeniably a fast man with a dollar, perpetually broke, but how is this tendency to be related to the bank affair? The testimony diverges at every point.

Even the facts that *are* known reflect this quandary. In July, 1895, a Grand Jury convened to investigate the embezzlement charge but found insufficient evidence to return an indictment. The case seemed to be closed, and Porter secured a position with the Houston *Post*, moving to that city for the few months he was employed. But the following February, thanks to the zealous determination of bank examiner F.B. Gray, who was apparently embittered over the initial ruling, the case was reopened, and this time Porter was indicted, with a trial set for July.

When July came, however, Porter did not. He did board the train from Houston, but whether with the resolve to go to Austin or not is yet another question, for somewhere in between he slipped off, ending up on a night coach bound for New Orleans.

No one except Porter himself has ever known for certain whether he was a guilty or innocent man and whether he actually intended to face his accusers when he left Houston. Years later he said to a friend in New York, referring to Joseph Conrad's book, "I am like Lord Jim, because we both made one fateful mistake at the supreme crisis of our lives, a mistake from which we could not recover."[27]

Whether that "mistake" was theft or flight, impulsive or premeditated, will remain forever a mystery, and consequently, so will Porter, to some extent. What matters now are the repercussions, for if he was believed by most people to be innocent—and indeed most friends felt he was—then flight only branded him otherwise and sealed his fate. But without this "mistake" and the fate it wrought, O. Henry would never have been born.

For several months Porter remained a fugitive, slipping from New Orleans to Honduras on a banana steamer, from thence on a ship bound around South America, ending up in Mexico City, San Diego, and finally Honduras again. All the while, he was observing, absorbing material which would later be transformed into the Louisiana and Latin America tales of *Cabbages and Kings* and *Roads of Destiny*. During his exile Porter remained secretly in touch with his family; when he was notified that his wife was in the final throes of her tuberculosis, he decided the game was up, and on February 5, 1897, he returned home. There he shared his last months with Athol until she died on July 25. The following February he stood trial, doing little to assist his case, refusing even to testify in his own defense. "He simply retreated into himself and let the lawyers fight it out."[28] He was found guilty, sentenced to five years—of which he would serve only three years, three months—and on April 25, 1898, he entered the Ohio Penitentiary, there to remain until July 24, 1901.

It is difficult to imagine how William Sydney Porter must have felt when he passed through the prison walls, fully expecting not to see freedom again for half a decade. The feeling would be tremulous for anyone, but for Porter, a shy, easygoing man, offended by profanity, who bore himself with an innate Southern dignity, the blow must have been intolerable. The early weeks were indeed desperate and depressed, with his letters tinged by suicidal inferences, though these threats were never followed through. John M. Thomas, the penitentiary's chief doctor, recalled, "In my experience of handling over ten thousand prisoners in the eight years I was physician at the prison, I have never known a man who was so deeply humiliated by his prison experience as O. Henry."[29]

Porter was lucky, though. His background as a pharmacist secured him an enviable job as night druggist, affording him a degree of solitude he treasured as well as time to write—which he did, every night. A later promotion to a position as secretary to the steward even permitted him to essentially live outside the prison walls, further easing the horror of confinement.

Nevertheless, the prison interregnum darkened Porter's life forever. He would never escape this relentless shadow of his past, and its haunting memory would infiltrate his later vision of life as well as affect the shape and substance of his stories.

For if Porter was already a reticent man, a dreamer and an onlooker, he became even more so in prison. He withdrew into himself as much as possible, making few friends, preserving the last remnants of his dignity but listening to and observing the plights and actions of other men.

He preferred to avoid involvement; he discouraged drawing any attention to himself, afraid to risk the slightest chance of having his sentence extended. Keeping clean and behaving, he no doubt felt, were his best bets. "He was a model prisoner," reported Dr. Thomas, "willing, obedient, faithful. His record is clear in every respect."[30]

This reticence extended even to situations of injustice worse than his own. On one occasion a fellow prisoner, an Indian, was presumed to be dead and was thrown into a trough; however, he was actually still alive and clawed his way out of the hole. Porter was sickened by the story but at the suggestion that he write about it he responded coldly, "I am not here as a reporter. I shall not take upon myself the burden of responsibility. This prison and its shame is nothing to me."[31]

Another time, a 17-year old boy was electrocuted for murder, only to be later found innocent. Again, angered as he was, Porter vented his feelings not in action but in words, observing rather than attempting to change the conditions. He blamed the wasted killing on "the viciousness of thought," which he considered a "curse" on the human race, said prison companion Al Jennings. "Certainly, if I did not think, I would be serenely contented tonight," Jennings quotes Porter. "I should not be dragged down with a ton weight of futile anger.... How can men sit on a jury and take into their hands such wicked power?"[32]

Porter's reluctance to probe too deeply or to become too involved might conceivably account—at least in part—for the lack of depth his later fictional characters display. This same reluctance to look too closely manifests itself in the stories; perhaps simply writing about conditions he deplored was sufficient "reform" for Porter. One biographer, in fact, accuses him of retreating "into the world of fiction" rather than confronting such wretched injustices.[33]

Nevertheless, despite his passivity, Porter's compassion for his fellow man and for victims of injustice was very real and was surely intensified by his own deep humiliation. As pharmacist, Porter had occasion to note the deplorable treatment afforded sick prisoners and to observe the indignities which men were forced to endure. "I never imagined human life was held as cheap as it is here," he wrote to his father-in-law. "The men are regarded as animals without soul or feeling."[34] This horror would register again later in New York on shopgirls, tenement dwellers, and other hapless victims, earning Porter the reputation as champion of the little man. But still he would remain the detached sympathizer, never the social reformer.

Besides, Porter too had become a victim. Like the wretches with whom he sympathized, he also had been forced into a role he did not wish to play, the role not only of "victim" but of "good prisoner," a performance calculated to ensure his prompt release. Porter's portrayal of the New York (and other) characters as types is no doubt influenced at least partly by seeing himself and others forced to conform to such roles. Though this tendency to perceive people as types had long been apparent, it was hardened into grim form by the criminal yoke. Outside prison, as one critic notes, "Porter's imagination touched again and again upon the routine playing of roles.... He seems never to have gotten the systematic pretense of the prison out of his system." Porter was labeled "thief" and "prisoner," and "his realization that society, at least in its institutional forms, cares more for the role than for the substance completes the reasons for the recurring examination of role and routine in O. Henry's works."[35]

Other consequences of imprisonment on Porter's later attitude and literary career are more immediately apparent than the psychological implications of his work. First of all, his literary career was launched from jail: in the free time provided by his coveted positions as druggist and private secretary, Porter wrote about a dozen of his best known stories and scattered his seeds in the marketplace by publishing a few, the first being "Whistling Dick's Christmas Stocking" in *McClure's* (December 1899). The writing process itself offered him an escape from the ugly, depressing environment, and his burning shame undoubtedly spurred him on in the desire to regain his integrity through literary and commercial success.

Second, the need to hide his identity and his past compelled Porter to seek another name. This was not a new tack, for he had assumed numerous pseudonymns before: Ten Eyck White (his first one), James Bliss, John Arbuthnot, S.H. Peters, and others. But now he took O. Henry as his permanent identity, a pen name destined to become almost as famous in American literature as Mark Twain. And just as Twain would be forever linked with Hannibal and the Mississippi River, so the name of O. Henry was to become inextricably associated with New York. Around this shadowy figure would be spun a kind of myth about the man who would reveal so little about himself.

Furthermore, the move itself to New York was propelled by Porter's convict trauma. When he emerged from prison, he wanted only to shut the door on the past forever. "I shall never mention the name of prison," he told Al Jennings. "I shall never speak of crime and punishments.... I will forget that I ever breathed behind these walls."[36]

The mythical O. Henry was born from the pain and strife of the prison years; without them he would never have existed. The fires of prison had forged the artist of the city.

When O. Henry passed out of the prison walls of Columbus he was a changed man. Something of the old buoyancy and waggishness had gone, never to return. He was never again to content himself with random squibs or jests contributed to newspapers or magazines. Creation had taken the place of mere scintillation. Observation was to be more and more fused with reflection. He was to work from the centre out rather than from the circumference in.[37]

New York held the promise of forgetfulness, for there Porter could submerge himself in the crowds of humanity. In the city, the fugitive could hide behind the writer, observer, and romantic known as O. Henry, a figure who would, through his peculiar vision and singular style, transform the crowded city into an exotic, enchanted realm distinctly his own.

When Porter emerged from prison in 1901, he emerged into a new century, one which "found the United States strong, prosperous, and confident."[38] Like Porter himself, the nation was in the throes of change, poised at the threshold of a new era.

Industrial development, a growing imperialism, the disappearance of the frontier, the 1893 Columbian Exposition's promise of a brave new world to come, Theodore Roosevelt's pronouncement that "the greatest victories are yet to be won, the greatest deeds yet to be done," all produced a spirit of energy and optimism, a shifting from provincialism to sophistication and internationalism, a readiness to renounce the past and embrace the future. America's "modern soul" had emerged, and a "mood of proud restlessness, of yearning for romance and adventure, became the dominant mood of the time...."[39]

The 1890s had been "a culmination;...the end of an era," a decade "dreamy with the past, yet alive with mighty gathering forces,...a decade of swift change."[40] It had been a time of certainty which Van Wyck Brooks labeled "The Confident Years." Now the new century burst in "like a tropic storm. All in a moment America woke to the fact that she was facing not only a new century, but a new era. Yesterday she was a world by herself, provincial and satisfied, built solidly upon Washington's Farewell Address...Now she was an empire...."[41]

Conflict, too, hung in the air: dissent was stirring over issues domestic and foreign; the gap was widening between the country's flock of millionaires and its struggling ranks of the poor; American society was growing more and more complex, with economic and political problems multiplying.[42] Overall, a measure of contradiction seemed to pervade the times:

The country was prosperous, smug, relaxed; prodigal in its generosity, hungry for novelty, ready for any ostentatious display, and eager for the kind of diversion appropriate to its new-found wealth. Under the surface there remained all the terrorism and uncertainty of life in the new epoch, the subterranean world that Frank Norris was soon to uncover in *McTeague*, Stephen Crane in *Maggie*, and Theodore Dreiser in *Sister Carrie*. On the surface, in a world busy digesting industrialism and the fruits of the Spanish-American War, it was the era of Richard Harding Davis and the Gibson Girl, of the rage for Stevenson and historical confectionary like George Barr McCutcheon's *Graustark* and Charles Major's *When Knighthood Was in Flower*.[43]

When Porter emerged into this heady, clamorous world, he too was a man divided, a walking contradiction, a man ending one era and facing a new one, yearning for this freedom yet fearful of the future. He bore a kind of kinship to the new century; in fact, Porter was in many respects a man of the times and for the times.

For one reason, Porter seemed to belong to the place in which he chose to begin his new life in 1902. The relationship appeared perfect: New York, with its roar and commotion, offered him the ideal refuge, a place where he could travel unnoticed, unquestioned, and lose himself in the masquerade. The heterogeneous array of people and the multi-faceted personality of this city, which in early 1900 still retained a rural charm, stirred his romanticism and nurtured his creative powers, so that he in turn endowed New York with a kind of immortality.

Porter was well-suited to the cultural and industrial temperament of the age as well. Mass production was in full swing and magazine circulation was booming, providing cheap and entertaining diversion for the hordes of workers flooding the cities. Porter's rapid and prolific pen turned out material perfectly suited to this literary industry; furthermore, he wrote about the very sorts of people who probably read him, the countless thousands whose lives were shaped and driven by the very technological forces which hastened Porter's own rise.

Historically, too, Porter became bound to his time. The birthing century would come to be known as "the age of O. Henry," for he was "a mirror held up to the period,"[44] and his influence on literature would reverberate through another decade as well.

Porter's relationship with New York City is akin to that of Twain and Missouri, Faulkner and Mississippi, Frost and New England: the two are inseparable. Though he wrote stories of the West and of South America, when one thinks of Porter—or at least

of O. Henry—one invariably associates him with New York, even
to the point of assuming he is its native. Conversely, for anyone
who has read Porter, it is difficult to picture New York without
conjuring up the flashing, thronging twilight bazaar that he
portrayed in his tales. O. Henry's New York possesses a timeless
quality, like a Robert Henri painting or an Alfred Stieglitz
photograph, conveying a real feeling of its charm, "its romance
and its multitudinous humanity and magic."[45] Two of Porter's
biographers even go so far as to suggest that his work, infused
as it is with the times, provides a sound historical basis for analyzing
the age. "Were all other records lost," write Davis and Maurice,
"from the forty-odd tales against the definite New York background
a future historian might rebuild a grotesque and alluring city that
would somehow be the city of that decade from 1900-1910, echoing
its voice, expressing the moods of its four million, and illuminating
its caliphs and its *cadis*. . . ."[46]

It is difficult to imagine any other place or time producing
such a remarkable symbiosis. Quite simply, "New York needed him
and he needed New York. . . . During the eight years of his stay . . . O.
Henry was to get closer to the inner life of the great city and to
succeed better in giving it a voice than anyone else had done. . . .
If ever in American literature the place and the man met, they met
when O. Henry strolled for the first time along the streets of New
York."[47]

Like Porter and like the new century, New York City was
experiencing its own changes in 1902. It had prospered during the
latter half of the nineteenth century, as the dominance of industry
generated a proliferation of vast urban centers all over America.
"In 1850 there had been only eighty-five cities with a population
of more than 8,000," but by 1900, "there were almost seven times
as many. The urban population doubled in the last two decades
of the century, rising to some thirty million. . . . This was the Age
of the Metropolis, and New York City was its leader, a financial,
commercial, and manufacturing center of well over three million."[48]

During this half century, the city was "an awakening giant
just beginning to be conscious of its strength," to shape its
personality,[49] and by the late 1890s it was fully conscious, flexing
its limbs, growing rapidly:

The first skyscrapers appeared as the city reached upwards. The city started to sprawl in all directions, with mass migrations to the Bronx, Brooklyn, and Staten Island. The Sixth and Ninth Avenue elevated railroads had been built, and the upper West Side began to lose its rural aspect.... It was evident now that Manhattan was becoming a vertical city; and Times Square was beginning to take shape as the amusement center of the city.[50]

Concurrent with this physical expansion was a swelling of the population and a concentration of a massive working class in the city, a pattern reflected all over America in the shift from rural to urban life. The lives of most of these people were marked by drudgery: routine, impersonal jobs and hectic, tiresome commutes "on the crowded 'els' or the horse-drawn trolleys."[51]

They sought diversion from this monotony, easy escape, craving to be "distracted from distraction by distraction,"[52] and so the demand for commercial entertainment grew. Considering that most workers were, by day's end, "too tired to do anything that required exertion," it's not too surprising that in the late 1890s New York "suddenly became a city of readers."[53] Reading material of all sorts was flourishing: dime novels, westerns, romances, adolescent libraries—and especially magazines.

This huge and eager public, combined with new advertising methods, technological advances in mass production, and cheaper prices, all made the *fin de siècle* a gold mine for the periodicals industry, providing conditions in which a writer like Porter could thrive. Never before had the low-priced magazine been so successful in American publishing.[54] In 1887 William Dean Howells commented on the magazine's "extraordinary development" as "nothing less than prodigious,"[55] and before the century's close, total periodical circulation had hit three million.[56]

As the century turned into the nineties, the creation of short periodical lengths had become well-nigh a profession. The age of magazines had opened...Magazines were soon to be advertised in terms of millions of subscribers, and every magazine was insistent in its demand for compelling tales. No literary product has ever swept from the presses in such floods. By the mid-nineties the production of the form had become a science, an art, an industry, with handbooks and schools and scholarly courses in the colleges.[57]

Porter wrote for several of the leading publications, including *McClure's*, which had published his first story, and *Ainslee's*, whose editors offered him his real break by providing the money for him to travel to New York. He landed a regular stint with the *New York World*, whose Sunday supplement was one of dozens which had sprung up to deflect the competition of magazines. The trend reflected also the increasing integration of journalism and literature as a journalistic passion swept through the late century, giving rise to "yellow journalism" and the spate of writers "trained in the mechanics of composition as no other had been in the history of literature."[58] Porter's clever and often mechanical style was distinctly compatible with this vogue, and his readers responded to him enthusiastically.

Another dominant trend by the end of the century was the growing popularity of fiction. An increase in short stories was one of the chief changes characterizing American magazines in the last quarter of the nineteenth century.[59] What the masses wanted, again, was pleasure: romance, adventure, vicarious experiences to compensate for the deficiencies of daily life. "The public expected of art not reality but a fantasy world to which it could escape. Readers were not yet ready for the realism of a Stephen Crane or a Frank Norris."[60]

But they *were* ready for Porter, whose bewitching tales turned on chance and circumstance and held the promise of adventure, while his surprise endings, though manipulated, offered a momentary if cheap thrill to his readers. He wrote of familiar figures—harried husbands, businessmen, working girls, policemen, tramps, and gangs; he mentioned recognizable places, streets and parks, uptown and downtown, Canfield's, Rooney's, dance-halls, the Bowery; and he alluded to numerous figures and events of the day such as Theodore Roosevelt and William Travers Jerome, touching all the while on the emotions, desires, and frustrations readers knew so well, and capturing the essence of the dazzling, crowded, tumultuous metropolis in which they lived.

Porter, of course, knew what would please his audience and he was able to provide it, a characteristic approach to the writing of the times. He was, in fact, "perfectly suited for readers of the 'all-fiction' press";[61] he was a popular artist (an identity which will be discussed more fully in the next chapter), a type of artist whose emergence is prompted by the development of a mass audience, especially one that is accessible through the mass media. "The popular artist had to make his own tradition by investigating the market, calculating its desires, and evolving devices...for reaching it. The popular artist became a kind of professional...who created for profit the kind of art that the public wanted."[62]

This is not to disparage the quality of popular art. While it is produced under certain restrictions—mainly the currents of popular taste, defined formats, and deadlines—it does demand certain skills, and within these limitations an artist can range from mechanical and undistinctive to talented and highly individual. Porter, as will be discussed later, left an indelible mark upon the work he produced. Though he leaned heavily upon formula and recognizable character types, he imbued them with a style that is distinctly his own. For Porter, formula provided a means to creativity, and he was occasionally even able to escape its limitations altogether.

Perhaps what was most appealing about Porter to his audience were the stories he spun—stories which infused fantasy into a familiar world and brought adventure within the ordinary man's grasp, just around the corner. Porter fulfilled the qualities of story-teller as delineated by Charles Agnew MacLean, one of the most distinguished editors in the heyday of popular magazines. To find stories in the world around him, said MacLean, requires a certain insight on the teller's part:

Life, as most of us see it in the raw, is a sort of confusion and disorder. Its rhythm and design are hidden from us. The story-teller catches up the tangled threads of many colors and casts them into a pattern of beauty and coherency; he discards the useless rubbish, and builds out of the broken fragments of experience the palace of our heart's desire....

A good author is a man who sees something interesting, romantic, noble and glamorous in the human drama that he fears others may miss. He wants them to see it too. He cannot be content to keep the vision to himself.[63]

Given Porter's skill and appeal as a storyteller, combined with the social and cultural conditions primed for his appearance, it is no wonder that his impact upon the early 1900s was tremendous, both during his life and after. He was, after Jack London, the "second original force that entered the new century"; by 1919, his publishers

would claim that well over four million of the author's books had
been sold, while for the next decade sales continued steadily.[64]

His career in New York was brief but brilliant: he arrived
suddenly and departed just as swiftly only a few years later, a comet
streaking through the literary skies. "The apparition of O. Henry
is the most extraordinary literary phenomenon of the new century,"
wrote Pattee in 1922. Like his contemporary Jack London, Porter
emerged "unheralded, full-grown, sudden: few arrivals in all
literature have been so startling. Hardly had we learned his real
name before he was filling the whole sky."[65]

That sky would extend "into a glorious evening that darkened
during the 1920s,"[66] but not before he had exerted notable influence
upon the short story as an art form. He instigated a widespread
obsession with manner and technique, and he sired a flock of would-
be imitators—Fannie Hursts and Edna Ferbers—who feverishly tried
to cash in on his formula. They were assisted by a host of compliant
teachers who reduced short story writing to a mechanical process
and, for better or for worse, acknowledged Porter as the
contemporary master of the form. Everywhere, O. Henryism—or
the O. Henry contagion, as Pattee dubbed it—prevailed:

Magazine fiction leaned heavily toward eccentricity of manner, up-to-dateness
of vocabulary and setting, smartness and unusualness in characterization and
in culminating paragraph.

In an age of standardization an elaborate attempt was made now to
standardize even fiction. The short story was made more and more a matter
of rules, of fixed requirements, of standard varieties and lengths like Ford
machines. These requirements filled dozens of handbooks and became the subject
matter even of correspondence courses. With all the standards and parts and
patterns thoroughly understood even the unliterary could make short stories.[67]

Whether one regards Porter's influence as remarkable or
distressing, his popularity cannot be denied, and that is the element
most responsible for making him an enduring figure in American
literature; in fact, a judgment of Porter as a writer hinges partly
on the judgment of popular art and literature in general.

Whether Porter could have met with such success in any other
time and place is of course impossible to know. But it is clear
that he was peculiarly a product of his times and for his times.
"To know O. Henry," wrote one critic, "is to know the age that

considered him a classic."[68] The turbulent, exciting tempo of the new century and the emerging city, the boom of mass production, and the astonishing quantity of magazines provided conditions well suited to Porter's needs and abilities, and his work in turn is infused with the times. So charmingly and memorably does he evoke the spirit and flavor of the age that it seems somehow to belong to him, so that in many respects this truly was the age of O. Henry.

Chapter Two
Porter and the Popular Tradition in Literature

As a popular artist, Porter shares company with a host of literary luminaries: Homer, Shakespeare, Twain, Hugo, Dickens, Melville, and innumerable others. Like them, he stirred the mass imagination, drawing for material from the world about him, probing the foibles, dilemmas, comedies, and tragedies of human existence, speaking in a voice that could be understood by the multitudes.

This communal kinship lies at the heart of Porter's popularity, as it does for any popular artist. The public could identify with and respond to the people, places, and situations Porter wrote about. His stories offered the escape from daily drudgery so desperately needed by "the four million" and fulfilled the fantasies—if only vicariously—they so often longed for. "The people of America loved O. Henry.... He was a nobody, but he was a nobody who was also a somebody, everybody's somebody."[1]

Porter, of course, calculated this success to some degree; he knew his audience and gave them what they wanted. "We have got to respect the conventions and delusions of the public to a certain extent," he wrote to his prison comrade Al Jennings. "In order to please John Wanamaker, we will have to assume a virtue that we do not possess."[2] Nevertheless, he perceived his subjects with a compassion and understanding that is unquestionably sincere. He specialized in humanity but did not exploit it. He accepted,

with a mixture of irony, wit, and sympathy, the distressing fact that a human being can be a clerk, the remarkable fact that a clerk can be a human being....

28

To O. Henry,...the clerk is neither abnormal nor subnormal. He writes of him without patronizing him. He realizes the essential and stupendous truth that to himself the clerk is not pitiable.[3]

Besides, Porter spins a good yarn, and he can turn a phrase as few authors ever have, rambling on in an easy, neighborly manner that slaps the reader on the shoulder, bandying an insouciant humor, and displaying a verbal range and precision that is astounding. He is a born raconteur; to listen to him is irresistible.

Above all, he is a master of technique. Even his severest critics acknowledge that as a designer of stories Porter "ranked supreme."[4] His manipulation of elements into a tight literary structure—a process which the next chapter will examine—is effective, if mechanical, and were one aspect of Porter's art to be held up as the most important or memorable, it would surely be this one.

He always has a story. The style or the mood may lure you away from it momentarily, but the tale always asserts its primacy, and its end comes always in just the whimsical way you didn't expect. O. Henry is inexhaustible in quip, in imagery, in quick, sharp spontaneous invention. In his apparent carelessness we suspect a carefulness, but this is just wherein he is sib to the French short-story writers, chief among them de Maupassant.[5]

All of these characteristics—his empathy for his fellow man, his sharp scrutiny of public demand, and his skill at the narrative craft—contribute to Porter's vast popularity. Furthermore, one other feature essential to popular art—wide-spread distribution—also accelerated Porter's rise to literary fame. As was discussed in the preceding chapter, the superfluity of magazines and the tremendous need for material were propitious conditions for the fledgling author; joined with his talents and the public's desire, they propelled Porter into a position as a popular and widely read writer.

In the decades since, his stories have been anthologized, collected, and reprinted; they have been translated into numerous foreign languages; they have been performed as radio, stage, and television drama, with some also made into films. Four of the most popular New York stories were combined into a movie entitled *O. Henry's Full House*: they were "The Last Leaf," "The Cop and the Anthem," "The Clarion Call," and "The Gift of the Magi," the last of which has itself become standard Yuletide fare for the populace, as popular and enduring as Dickens' *A Christmas Carol*. "True to the style of the author, who was right in the popular groove," wrote one film reviewer about this movie, "it is a compact and varied entertainment—brisk, direct, and tricked with the element of surprise.... Notable in all of these episodes is a flavor and atmosphere of New York when it was Bagdad on the Subway and O. Henry was grinding out his tales."[7]

Such broad appeal is the domain of the popular artist, be he author, musician, performer, painter, or other creative type. Although he manifests a style distinctly his own and is recognizable by his particular manner, the popular artist conforms to certain expectations, presenting his material in forms familiar to his audiences and mirroring the joys and frustrations, the excitement and ennui of their everyday lives. This direct, personal relationship is one which the popular artist strives for, aiming deliberately to reach and to please his readers or listeners. Unlike "elite" or "high" art, which springs from individual and aesthetic motives, or folk art, which tends to be anonymous and utilitarian, popular art purposely appeals to the masses, while displaying the unmistakable touch of a single creator.

Popular art, aimed at the majority, is neither abstruse, complicated, or profound [sic]. To understand and appreciate it should require neither specialized, technical, nor professional knowledge. It is relatively free of corrective influences derived from minority sources; its standards of comprehension and achievement are received from consensus; it must be commonly approved, pervasive in the population, "popular" in the sense that the majority of people like and endorse it and will not accept marked deviations from its standards and conventions. More individualized than folk art, but less so than elite, popular art tends to be more dependant than either on the skill of the performer.[8]

The skills of Porter as popular performer fuse into a style as distinctive and memorable as Charlie Chaplin's or Alfred Hitchcock's, an indelible style which breathes "O. Henryism" into his tales. Two of the most predominant components of this style—the two which will be explored in the following chapters—are plot structures and character types. The most famous and easily recognized plot characteristic is, of course, the surprise ending, a trick which results from clever, careful strategy. Although Porter was certainly not the first writer to employ this device—de Maupassant being particularly inclined toward it—he popularized it and staked a peculiar claim upon it, so that it has come to be inextricably linked with him and dubbed "the O. Henry twist." In terms of characters, the most well-known is probably the shopgirl, a type which, again, is invariably associated with the writer.

Other idiosyncrasies also contribute to the "O. Henryism" that generated such enthusiastic response: the folksy narrative voice, confidential asides to the reader, intricate and sometimes outrageous language and dialogue, full-blown metaphors, hyperbole, and copious allusions.[9]

Porter embroiders all these elements together to form a personal style that distinguishes his work from that of other popular writers, even though such writers may employ similar or identical devices. Less skillful popular artists may depend so heavily upon story formula or character stereotypes to accomplish their purposes that individual artistry is obliterated; indeed, a whole slew of nineteenth-century fiction manufacturers churned out material in such quantity and such anonymity that their work "was more or less comparable to the product of machines,"[10] and authors were easily interchangeable—names like Horatio Alger, Jr., Laura Jean Libbey, Edward Stratemeyer, and Edward Judson pertain.[11] But a popular artist like Porter is an essential creative force behind his products; his shaping hand is always apparent, and his presence within his work helps to establish the rapport so important to the popular artist. As one critic points out, "To read him is at times almost to feel his physical presence."[12]

This unique style, a compilation of several elements, defines Porter's work internally as well as externally. Besides setting him apart from other popular writers, Porter's style constitutes a kind of formula which recurs within and defines his own body of work. This evolution of a personal, recognizable formula is intrinsic to popular art: "the quality of stylization and convention" that is so important "becomes a kind of stereotyping, a processing of experience, a reliance upon formulae."[13] In other words, the artist employs his selected materials—characters, settings, plots, etc.—over and over again, so that they become familiar aspects within his work, yet he also imbues them with a flavor distinctly his own.

In popular literature, these materials are already known to the audience: a character type such as the hero or outcast; a setting such as a town or a home; a plot such as boy meets girl, boy loses girl, boy gets girl back; and so forth. But the skilled popular artist will transform these commonplace elements into a story (or film, performance, etc.) that bears his unmistakable imprint or signature, so that the final product is partly original, partly standardized, a happy marriage of a singular vision and routine materials. "For the popular artist, stylization is necessary, and the conventions provide an agreed base from which true creative invention springs.... The popular artist may use the conventions to select, emphasize and stress (or alter the emphasis and stress) so as to delight the audience with a kind of creative surprise."[14]

This is the creative balance which Porter strikes in his art. Working within a recognizable set of conventional story patterns and character types, Porter evolves, along with other particular stylistic aspects, his own recurring set of patterns and his own unique array of individuals who are at once distinctive and universal.

What will be examined in the following two chapters, which together form the core of this study, are these two elements—plot patterns and character types—so central to Porter's individual style, with a consideration both of how they help to define Porter's work externally, as popular literature, as well as how, by repetition, they define his body of work internally.

In a sense, because of the personal style that emerges through his recurrent use of specific literary elements, Porter can be considered an *auteur*, and the proposal to examine his body of work in terms of these elements is essentially the approach of *auteur* criticism. Originating in the 1950s as a mode of film criticism,[15] the *auteur* theory offers a worthwhile model for analyzing and interpreting popular culture in general, as John Cawelti suggests in his seminal essay on the subject:

The art of the *auteur* is that of turning a conventional and generally known and appreciated artistic formula into a medium of personal expression while at the same time giving us a version of the formula which is satisfying because it fulfills our basic expectations.[16]

For a popular artist like Porter, the *auteur* approach, with its emphasis on surveying an entire body of material to discover and analyze structural characteristics and stylistic motifs, seems particularly appropriate and useful. What is distinctive about *auteur* criticism is that it stresses "the whole *corpus*"[17] of material rather than a single work, emphasizing recurring characteristics and themes; it "implies an operation of decipherment"[18] and ultimately defines the *auteur*—the filmmaker, the author—in terms of these recurring elements, which come to be recognized as his particular style. "The strong director imposes his own personality on a film,"[19] just as a writer can stamp his distinctive seal on his own creations.

Although the *entire* body of Porter's work is not under consideration here, an important core of his canon is. The New York stories form a singular portion of his literary output for several reasons: together, they comprise well over a third of his work; they are bound together by their urban characteristics; they were produced during the most significant period of his literary career; and they include most of the stories for which he is so well remembered. Furthermore, the recurring characteristics and themes which are discovered here through "an operation of decipherment" can then serve as models for examining Porter's other stories—of Texas, New Orleans, and South America—which display similar structural and character motifs though in different cultural contexts.

As a popular artist, Porter is similar to the type of filmmaker who emerges in *auteur* criticism, since the latter is essentially a cinematic popular artist. Both the *auteur* and the popular artist utilize formulaic elements of plot and character to create a personal, recognizable style, weaving new variations on old familiar themes. Both, in turn, develop this individual style into a kind of personal formula running through their work. Both are also confronted by similar restrictions—mainly, conventional limitations on characters, setting, and plots, and commercial demands in their given mediums. "All directors," notes Andrew Sarris, "and not just in Hollywood, are imprisoned by the conditions of their craft and their culture."[20]

So the identities of these two creative types are similar: like the popular artist, the *auteur* is neither absolutely original nor completely technical; rather, like the popular artist, he is an individual creator who works within a framework of existing materials, conventional structures created by others, but he is more than a performer because he recreates those conventions to the point that they manifest at least in part the patterns of his own style and vision.[21]

The *auteur* approach, then—for filmmakers, for a popular writer like Porter, and for other popular artists as well—focuses on "an examination of the entire body of work for recurrent stylistic and thematic patterns rather than the isolated analysis of the individual work in its unique totality."[22] It is similar to the approach taken in this study, although the focus here is on a significant and representative group of stories rather than the *entire* body of Porter's work. The patterns that will be examined in the plots and characters of Porter's urban stories draw upon conventional situations, reinforce conventional values and expectations, and embody recognizable cultural types. By occurring repeatedly within the body of Porter's work, these plots and characters define it internally; by emulating more universal, archetypal patterns and characters, they achieve a broader recognition and a similarity to other artistic products, while remaining distinctive to Porter's art.

This continual recurrence of specific motifs, so central to Porter's art, to popular art, and to the theory of *auteur* criticism, constitutes the element of formula. For Porter, as for any popular artist, formula provides the fundamental structure for his art, and not surprisingly, it also contributes to his popular appeal. For as a constant and predictable pattern, formula is inherent to the cycle of human existence, and it also characterizes the earliest forms of literature most people learn—myths, fairy tales, songs, etc. Because it is so elemental, formula is familiar and comforting; it is an artistic expression of the subliminal human need for security and certainty in a life that promises just the opposite, and to some extent at least, the presence of formula in popular literature satisfies that need.

"High" or "elite" art, unlike popular or even folk art, lacks these elements of predictability and standardization, so that popular art is, by and large, the type most accessible to the ordinary individual, relating more closely to the experiences of everyday life and to the rhythms of existence.

In his important study *Adventure, Mystery and Romance: Formula Stories As Art and Popular Culture,* John Cawelti defines a literary formula as, in general, "a structure of narrative or dramatic conventions employed in a great number of individual works." This is a broad, encompassing definition, but in it Cawelti sets forth the two major elements of formulaic literature: convention and repetition.

The first major element is convention. As opposed to invention, which refers to original creations, convention denotes elements familiar to both the author and the reader. Conventions "consist of things like favorite plots, stereotyped characters, accepted ideas, commonly known metaphors and other linguistic devices, etc."[24] While inventions, Cawelti says, confront us with new, previously unrecognized perceptions, "conventions represent familiar shared images and meanings and they assert an ongoing continuity of value."[25] Conventions therefore may be cultural elements and thus be limited in their effect to a particular time, place, and people, or they may be universal and thus transcend such limitations. Or they may be fusions of these two aspects, with the universally held conventions being presented in terms of a specific cultural convention; thus, for example, Porter may present the familiar, universal character of the outcast in the cultural garb of the tramp, a figure who will, in turn, also be shaped by certain expectations. These two aspects of convention are equivalent to the more familiar terms "archetype" and "stereotype," the only difference between them being the range of their focus and the extent of their appeal.

Cawelti makes the same kind of distinction in defining formula, breaking the term down into two usages which, taken together, adequately define a literary formula. The first usage of the term, he says, "denotes a conventional way of treating some specific thing or person," such as Homer's epithets, standard similes and metaphors; and by extension, "any form of cultural stereotype commonly found in literature."[26] What is important about this usage is its limited nature: "it refers to patterns of convention which are usually quite specific to a particular culture and period and do not mean the same outside this specific context."[27] Porter's shopgirl, for example, who assumes specific characteristics as a type within the context of the stories, is a conventional embodiment of the innocent, vulnerable orphan, the same kind of role a young male

Dickens character might play. But removed from Porter's stories or from the context of America's social and industrial conditions in the early twentieth century, the shopgirl would not convey the same meaning, while in the literature of another time or culture, the character of the shopgirl may assume different characteristics altogether from those she displays in Porter's stories. As Boris Ejxenbaum points out, "Tender stories about New York shopgirls have more appeal for the American reader" than for Russian readers.[28]

The second usage of the term "formula" encompasses larger plot types, which are not limited to specific cultures. Rather, these plot patterns "seem to represent story types that, if not universal in their appeal, have certainly been popular in many different cultures at many different times."[29] They are, in other words, archetypal patterns: the adventure story, the romance, and the quest are three examples.

The fusion of these two usages—that is, the "synthesis of a number of specific cultural conventions with a more universal story form or archetype"[30]—constitutes a formula. Put another way, formula can be defined as "a conventional system for structuring cultural products."[31]

The other major element of formula, repetition, involves, like the term "convention," distinctions of degree. Within the context of one author's work—in this case Porter's urban short stories—repetition involves the frequency with which the author employs specific plot patterns and specific cultural elements. It is through such repetition that the works assume a formulaic nature. For example, Porter's cross-purposes plot (which is explained in the following chapter) could hardly be construed as an element of his formulaic art if he used it only once, nor could the shopgirl evolve into a stereotype if she made only one appearance in the stories. It is the element of repetition which causes the standardization of particular products, thus enabling them to become familiar to the readers.

Secondly, repetition involves the frequency with which the plot patterns and cultural elements have been employed outside the context of the author's works. This is the universal aspect of repetition and the means by which plot patterns and specific elements become archetypal and serve as models of comparison for specific works. The existence of a universal story pattern, or of a general element such as a character type defined only by human traits, not bounded by cultural details, provides the standard of comparison for an author's works and the framework on which he can, with specific cultural elements, construct a story which will be relevant and meaningful to a certain group of people in a certain place and time.

Elements of repetition are quite apparent in Porter's urban short stories, for he draws recurringly upon a number of basic plot patterns and character types. Variations occur, of course, and not every single story can be neatly categorized according to plot and character; such extremism threatens to squeeze the life out of the literature. Still, in the nearly one hundred stories that deal with the city, recurrent plot patterns and characters do emerge which can be identified and used as a means of classification.

The plots of these stories can be divided into four basic patterns, overlapping to some extent but nevertheless bearing distinguishing characteristics: they are the cross pattern, the habit pattern, the triangular pattern, and the quest pattern. All develop themes familiar to most readers: the cross pattern, for example, builds on the unexpected reunion; the habit pattern provides excitement by an unexpected change in routine; the triangular pattern inserts a new twist in the familiar love triangle, and the quest pattern is Porter's version of the adventure story. As Chapter Three illustrates, Porter repeatedly uses these patterns, or some variation of them, in his stories.

The characters, too, can be divided into six basic types, although because they often play more than one role simultaneously, they are more difficult to classify definitively. These six types—the shopgirl, the habitual character, the lover, the aristocrat, the plebeian, and the tramp—are examined in Chapter Four. Each type is a composite of specific characteristics, such as appearance, lifestyle, and attitude—characteristics which identify the entire group, with little if any attention paid to individual tendencies. Furthermore, each character type responds to conventional expectations: the shopgirl is poor but brave; the habitual character sticks to the ordinary routine of domestic life; the lover places love above self-interest; the aristocrat places money below principle; the plebeian bears the standard marks of poverty; and the tramp sleeps on a park bench.

Thus, Porter draws upon a "conventional system" for structuring his stories. His plot patterns are formulaic within the context of his own works, for he uses a number of patterns repeatedly; they are also formulaic in their relationship to more standard universal models. His characters are formulaic because they appear repeatedly, as types, within the stories and also because they represent, underneath their garb of culture, more universal character types. This recurrence of character type and plot pattern, and the interweaving of specific cultural material with more universal standards, together form the basis of the formulaic art of Porter's urban short stories.

Chapter Three
Plot Patterns

By virtue of its recurrent nature, a plot pattern is an essential element of formulaic art in fiction. The plots of Porter's urban short stories fall into four basic patterns: the cross pattern, the habit pattern, the triangular pattern, and the quest pattern. As used here, the term "plot pattern" refers to the basic structural elements which constitute each particular type of plot, though these basic patterns, as the chapter will illustrate, are subject to a number of variations within their defined frameworks.

I

The plot pattern which Porter employs most frequently, and the one most discussed and referred to by critics, is what can be called the cross pattern. This pattern is characterized by certain specific elements, but because of variations in these elements, it will be further divided into three sub-patterns: cross-purposes, crossed-paths, and cross-identity. In the cross pattern, the surprise ending occurs at the point where two paths travelled by characters in the story intersect, seemingly unexpectedly; however, closer examination reveals that usually this crossing was on the map all along, though so small and remote as to be easily overlooked. This intersection is the significant element in the cross formula, and Porter maneuvers his characters toward it via three separate routes.

The first route is the widely known and discussed pattern of cross-purposes. Here a central problem which induces the entire action of the plot presents itself at the outset. Generally the dilemma is financial, demanding action by one or both of the characters involved, who are united at the story's opening, split to pursue independent paths, and reunite at the close. The core of the plot is this: two characters are simultaneously working to solve some problem, each one unaware of the other's efforts; however, when they unite at the end and discover one another's strategies, it turns out that one individual's actions have in some way affected the other's, with the result usually being that both actions are cancelled out so that the characters have unwittingly been working against, or at cross-purposes to, one another. There are exceptions, though, and the outcome isn't necessarily futile, for the irony of the situation can serve to reinforce the relationship between the two characters.

The story which most vividly illustrates this pattern is also the most well-known of all Porter's tales, "The Gift of the Magi," which James Douglas considers "perhaps the finest tabloid story in literature."[1] Set in an eight-dollar-a-week New York City furnished flat on Christmas Eve day, the story centers around an impoverished young couple surviving on little more than love. Each of these "children," as Porter calls them, has one prize possession which both cherish: Della's long, lustrous hair, and Jim's heirloom gold watch. At the opening, Della is lamenting the insufficiency of the $1.87 she has managed to scrape together for Jim's Christmas present. Struck by sudden inspiration, she rushes out and sells her hair for $20; with the money, she buys Jim a handsome watch fob, then returns home to nervously await his arrival. When he comes and beholds Della's close-cropped curls, he reacts with a kind of shock, the result, one would assume, of his wife's transformation. But the real reason for his astonishment soon becomes apparent: he has bought Della the set of beautiful combs which she had for so long admired in a Broadway window. Della, eagerly insisting that her hair will soon grow back, then presents him with the watch chain, whereupon Jim informs her that he has sold the watch in order to buy the combs.

This story is recounted from Della's point of view. The reader observes her actions, aware that she is selling her most prized possession in order to enhance Jim's, but unaware that Jim is following the same course of action, for the same motives. Jim's half of the picture is eclipsed by Porter's deft handling of the plot, and only when the two courses of action intersect—that is, when Della and Jim meet at the end of the day and exchange gifts—do we see the other half of the picture and learn the sadly humorous irony that results.

Blance Williams illustrates this plot pattern as a mathematical design:

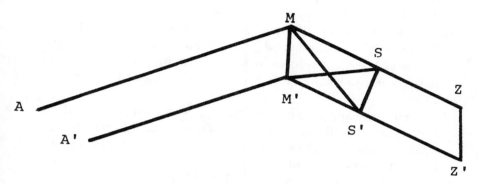

(Figure 1, Cross-Purposes)

That is, at M Della sells her hair; at S she buys the fob; at M' Jim sells his watch; at S' he buys the combs.

There is a direct link between M and S' (the selling of the hair and the buying of the combs), and between M' and S (the selling of the watch and the buying of the fob). It is this connection which labels such a story as one of "crosspurposes."

It should be noted that in the story *presentation*, only the denouement reveals that the previous "cross" exists.

AZ represents Della's struggle, in which she is successful; A' Z' represents Jim's struggle, in which he is successful. The climax of action for each is the presentation of the gifts.[2]

The ending of the story is marked by Porter's characteristic double twist: having sprung one surprise on his reader, he fires off a second before the reader has time to recover from the first. The initial surprise here is Della's discovery that Jim has bought the revered set of combs for her now-shorn hair, thus rendering his gift useless; the follow-up is Jim's revelation that he has sold his watch, thus rendering Della's gift useless. Both stages of this twist ending lead to the same consequence.

Though this clever ending is generally startling, for the seasoned, astute O. Henry reader it is not altogether unexpected, since clues woven subtly into the tale point directly to the pre-planned crossing of paths. The first clue is only implied, but pretty clearly. Since Della is bemoaning her meagre $1.87 savings, despite months of scrimping and "bulldozing the grocer and the vegetable man and the butcher,"[3] it is logical to conclude that James Dillingham Young finds himself in the same financial grip, feeling the same yearning to buy her something special for Christmas.

The second clue is even more obvious: when we are told that Della's hair is her pride and joy and could have depreciated the Queen of Sheba's jewels, we also learn that Jim's watch, his prize possession, could have made King Solomon pluck his beard with envy.

The third and crucial clue is handed to us when Della sacrifices her treasured hair for the watch chain. The plot has thus far followed a parallel pattern: both Della and Jim love each other dearly, implied through exposition; both are poverty-stricken on Christmas Eve; both own a treasured possession. Thus, when one sells her treasure to buy a gift which will enhance the other's treasure, it is logical to assume that the other character will act likewise, in keeping with the parallel pattern. The other character does, and it is here that the crossing is determined. At this point they symbolically cross paths by performing an action for the purpose of pleasing the other, and this symbolic crossing is revealed in the final, real crossing that occurs when they exchange gifts.

Thus, the story develops in four main stages: the problem is presented, one character pursues a solution, the actual crossing occurs, and the cross-purpose action of the symbolic encounter is revealed.

A slightly different version of this cross-pattern underlies "A Service of Love." The situation and characters are cast from the same mold as "The Gift of the Magi": the young husband and wife, Joe and Delia, are pursuing artistic careers—he in painting, she in music; again, the problem is a shortage of money. Delia insists on engaging pupils and one night proudly announces that she has been hired as tutor for the frail daughter of a wealthy Colonel at $15 per week. Shortly afterwards, Joe reveals that he has sold a watercolor for $18, with a commission to paint more.

A week later, Delia arrives home one evening with her hand and wrist bandaged, complaining that her student spilled hot Welsh rabbit on her after the lesson. When she explains that the Colonel had sent someone, "the furnace man or somebody in the basement" (27) for oil and bandages, Joe insists on knowing the truth. After an initial denial, Delia confesses that she had never been giving piano lessons at all but working in a shirt laundry, where a girl had accidentally set an iron down on her. Joe then admits that he had sent up oil and cotton from the engine room where he has been working to a girl upstairs who had burnt her hand; there had never been any customers for his paintings.

Like "Gift," this story is told from the woman's viewpoint, though this time even her side is partially eclipsed also. The pattern of action is also the same: the initial problem, caused by lack of money, is presented; one character—again, the wife—devises a solution but actually develops a separate one which neither husband nor reader is aware of. Simultaneously, the husband discovers a means of easing the financial crisis, but he too is covering up the real intention. In this case, the two deceivers may have been able to maintain their pretenses indefinitely but for the untimely and convenient crossing of paths when Jim sends up oil and cloth, unaware that the girl who needs these materials is his wife.

This crossing, like the first, symbolic crossing in "Gift," is revealed through flashback; it is not a primary action in the plot. At the time it occurs it is not significant, for neither Joe nor Delia is aware of it. Not until the second crossing, when Joe and Delia meet at home that night, does this initial meeting become apparent and thus significant, providing the story's twist.

Again, Porter employs the double surprise device: the first to reveal Delia's masquerade, the second to reveal Jim's. Unlike "Gift," however, these two stages do not cancel each other out; neither of the characters' services is rendered useless because of the other's action, though the motivation is similar.

And again, the ending is not a complete surprise to the sharp-eyed reader. The same parallel pattern unfolds: both characters are deeply in love and both are dedicated to their careers. (In fact, they meet in an atelier where art and music students gather to talk.) Delia is the first to provide an income from her art, but Joe is not long in following. At the end of the first week of "lessons," Delia lays her fifteen dollars on the table; then Joe drops his eighteen from his "painting." Further, we are told that he is off at seven every morning to make sketches in Central Park, not coming home until seven at night.

We receive a second hint when one night, Joe arrives home first, spreads his $18 on the table, and then "washed what seemed to be a great deal of dark paint from his hands" (27); a while later, Delia arrives with her bandaged wrist. Once she admits to her real occupation, it is only a quick step to the conclusion that Joe is guilty of a similar deception. The thread which binds this double deception, however, suffers from a weakness not present in "Gift": the element of chance. It is sheer coincidence that Delia works in a shirt factory located in the very same building as the engine room where Jim is employed, thus enabling their paths to cross. No such loose thread mars "Gift."

The cross-purposes plot pattern thus develops in four stages: first, the presentation of the problem, usually financial, along with some exposition on the characters' relationship; second, the course of action one character pursues, motivated by love; third, the final, fateful encounter, the crossing of paths, with the revelations that trigger the fourth stage, in which the other character's action is exposed, along with the initial crossing of paths. The first stage of the double twist coincides with her revelation, the second with his.

Stripped to its bare structure the pattern looks like this: complication—pursuit of solution—encounter (cross) with other character—revelation of conflicting solution and of initial crossing of paths. Using this framework, Porter constructs a variety of story forms, not all of which incorporate the husband—wife—poverty—love cycle.

Take, for example, "The Love Philtre of Ikey Schoenstein," built upon the cross-purposes pattern but with some story elements altered, though the element of unknown conflict remains. The two main characters are Ikey, a night clerk at the Blue Light Drug Store, and Chunk McGowan, his friend and also amorous rival, since both are in love with Rosy Riddle, proverbial daughter of Ikey's boardinghouse landlady. The unfortunate Ikey, however, is timid with the opposite sex, "a weak-kneed, purblind, motorman-cursed rambler" (50), while Chunk "picked them off the bat" (50).

One afternoon, Chunk gleefully announces that he and Rosy are to elope that night, provided that Rosy doesn't change her mercurial mind and that her father doesn't smell a rat. The bridegroom enlists Ikey's aid, imploring him to concoct a drug to enamor Rosy of him and keep her from "reneging on the proposition to skip" (52). Ikey, while pretending to assent, actually mixes a sleeping powder of morphia; furthermore, after Chunk leaves, he informs Rosy's father of the secret affair.

All night long, Ikey awaits news of his rival's defeat. At eight the next morning, when the day clerk arrives, Ikey speeds off for the boarding house, but as he whisks out the door he encounters Chunk stepping from a car, flushed with victory:

> "The—the—powder?" stammered Ikey.
>
> "Oh, that stuff you gave me!" said Chunk, broadening his grin; "well, it was this way. I sat down at the supper table last night at Riddle's, and I looked at Rosy, and I says to myself, 'Chunk, if you get the girl get her on the square—don't try any hocus-pocus with a thoroughbred like her. And I keeps the paper you give me in my pocket. And then my lamps fall on another party present, who, I says to myself, is failin' in a proper affection toward his comin' son-in-law, so I watches my chance and dumps that powder in old man Riddle's coffee,—see?" (53)

The plot variations here occur in three areas: the characters, the complication, and the viewpoint. The key characters are two men instead of a man and a woman; the complication, which concerns love rather than poverty, is actually twofold, with the rivalry between the young men as well as the double handicap faced by the leading contender; finally, the viewpoint this time is a man's, but as in "Gift," we still receive a valuable piece of inside information—the morphia—which enables us to appreciate Ikey's stunned surprise.

Following the complication, both characters pursue solutions, ostensibly parallel courses (but actually not), leading to the crucial juncture and the double twist. The initial surprise is Chunk's success; the second, his revelation of slipping the powder to Mr. Riddle, reveals the hidden conflict of solutions, the previous crossing of paths. Motivation is again the key: Chunk ethically changes his mind at the last minute, just as Ikey had jealously sabotaged his friend's plan, the outcome being that each solution cancels out the other, though not so flawlessly as in "Gift." (An obvious weakness here is that even if Chunk had administered the *intended* potion to Rosie's father, the outcome would most likely have been the same.)

Innumerable such variations can be explored, but the basic pattern of the cross-purposes plot remains the same: complication—pursuit of solution—cross—revelation of conflicting solution and initial cross.

The second route by which Porter steers his characters toward the hidden crossroads can be labeled the crossed-paths pattern. Again, this pattern hinges completely on the fateful, literal intersection of two characters' paths; and again, the final encounter balances out a previous one, occurring before the divergence of paths and usually before the story opens. But unlike the cross-purposes pattern, the characters do not turn out to be counteractive. Instead, the emphasis here is on divergence: two characters are separated; the action concerns their attempt to locate each other, and the final crossroads marks their reunion. The big city, with its vastness and impersonality, often acts as antagonist to this reunion.

The structure of the pattern is this: initial encounter (mentioned or implied early in the story but not occurring in the story)—divergence of paths (usually unavoidable)—complication (the foiled reunion)—chance occurrence (known or hidden)—final encounter, with the usual twist and surprising revelation.

"Tobin's Palm," the opening story in *The Four Million*, offers a clever and imaginative illustration of the crossed-paths pattern. John, the narrator, reveals the complication at the outset to explain why he and Tobin are seeking distraction at Coney Island: "For there was Katie Mahorner, his sweetheart, of County Sligo, lost since she started for America three months before with $200, her own savings, and $100 from the sale of Tobin's inherited estate, a fine cottage and pig on the Dog Shannaugh" (1).

At the amusement park, Tobin has his palm read by Madame Zozo, who informs him that he has been in love, that trouble has come from this love, and that his sweetheart's initials are K.M.; she then warns him to beware of a dark man and a light woman and predicts that he will make a voyage upon water and suffer a financial loss, and that a crooked-nosed man with a long name will bring him good luck.

Tobin, a firm believer in such foretellings, is delighted, and with "Jawn," as he calls his friend, he heads back to the ferry. On the boat, "a nigger man sticks his lighted segar against Tobin's ear, and there is trouble" (3); in the commotion, Tobin's pockets are emptied; he accidentally kicks the foot of a young woman "with hair the color of an unsmoked meerschaum" (3), and in attempting to apologize, he starts to tip his hat but the wind whips it off. Suddenly, Tobin realizes that they are taking a journey upon the water and excitedly tells "Jawn" that all these occurrences correspond to the predictions. Immediately he begins to look for the crooked-nosed man; when they alight and walk uptown, Tobin spots him beneath a streetlamp, a long man with a nose which "made two twists from bridge to end, like the wriggle of a snake" (4). Accosting him, Tobin learns that his name is Maximus G. Friedenhausman and tries to extract his predicted good luck. The man is disconcerted, but Tobin stubbornly refuses to be shaken off. After learning from "Jawn" that Tobin is simply under the influence of a fortune teller, he takes them into a saloon for a few drinks, then hospitably invites them to his home for some refreshment.

" 'I will ask the new girl we have in the kitchen,' says he, 'to make ye a pot of coffee to drink before ye go. 'Tis fine coffee Katie Mahorner makes for a green girl just landed three months. Step in,' says the man, 'and I'll send her down to ye' " (7).

The initial encounter here is Katie and Tobin's implied union in Ireland; the divergence occurs when Tobin leaves for America; the complication sets in when Katie, upon her arrival, becomes lost in the depths of the city. Tobin's fruitless search for her leads him to the fortune teller, who proves to be the catalyst to the final meeting, abruptly turning Tobin's path in the direction of Katie's; somewhere in the vast city, Katie is presumably pursuing a similar search. Thus far the story follows the parallel pattern of the cross-purposes plot.

However, in this case the final crossing does not reveal any previous conflict or unknown encounter. The discovery of the lost sweetheart constitutes the surprise element, and like the initial union, it is implied but not actually depicted, since the story stops just short of the actual crossing. Had Porter continued, he conceivably could have woven some such cross-purpose into the twist, but he didn't, and this absence, compounded by the lost and found theme, differentiates this pattern from the cross-purposes.

One variation of the crossed-paths pattern involves concealing the chance element until the end of the story, as in "Springtime À La Carte." Sarah, a poor rooming-house waif, ekes out a living by freelancing with her typewriter; with some ingenuity, she has managed to persuade Schulenberg's Home Restaurant next door to pay her three meals a day for typing their daily menus neatly onto cards. As the story opens, spring is approaching but Sarah is unhappy, for the farmer's son whom she had fallen in love with the previous summer, and who had promised they would wed at the first signs of spring, has not yet arrived. The seasonal changes are reflected in the menu she is typing, with the vegetables including an egg dish with dandelions. When Sarah spots this entry, the memories of her dandelion-entwined summer and the benighted lover rush upon her, and she drops her head upon the typewriter to weep. Finally, drawing herself up, she finishes and delivers the menus. Later that evening, she hears a knock downstairs, pauses to listen, and in a moment her farmer rushes up the stairs. He has been roaming the city for a week, unable to find her; by chance he drops into the Home Restaurant next door and discovers the clue to her whereabouts:

"...When I got below cabbage I turned my chair over and hollered for the proprietor. He told me where you lived."

"I remember," sighed Sarah, happily, "That was dandelions below cabbage."

"I'd know that cranky capital W 'way above the line that your typewriter makes anywhere in the world," said Franklin.

"Why, there's no W in dandelions," said Sarah in surprise.

The young man drew the bill of fare from his pocket and pointed to a line.

Sarah recognized the first card she had typewritten that afternoon. There was still the rayed splotch in the upper right-hand corner where a tear had fallen. But over the spot where one should have read the name of the meadow plant, the clinging memory of their golden blossoms had allowed her fingers to strike strange keys.

Between the red cabbage and the stuffed green peppers was the item: "DEAREST WALTER, WITH HARD-BOILED EGG." (62)

Here the twist ending holds the clue which turns Walter's path towards Sarah's, a move which actually is sealed the moment Sarah weeps on her card and types the propitious error. But the reader gets no hint of this mistake, so its importance is unknown until the end. This shift of emphasis is the variation Porter works on the basic crossed-paths pattern: there are the initial encounter, split, and promised reunion, all revealed in exposition; again, the city stymies this meeting, complicated by Walter's not having received Sarah's letters (for some unexplained reason); both characters follow a parallel course of seeking one another; finally, some chance element—in this case the mis-typed menu—turns one course in the direction of the other and toward the important crossroads.

This omission of a significant step, which is found in other Porter stories as well, is cited by Blanche Williams as one of several possible formulaic plot arrangements. She illustrates this one alphabetically, so that a step relocated from the regular order of events, placed after the climax, would read like this: ABCDEFGHIJKLMQRSTUVWXYZNOP.[4]

A peculiar variation on the crossed-paths pattern occurs in the controversial story "The Furnished Room," one of the few stories with sad rather than happy endings.[5] As in the other tales, the action of "The Furnished Room" culminates in an intersection of paths, wherein lies the story's twist; however, this meeting is symbolic and spiritual rather than literal and physical, an unusual variation that lends a haunting quality to the story.

The action focuses on a young man who is prowling the crumbling red brick boarding houses of the lower West Side in search of the girl he loves, who apparently has come to New York with dreams of a singing career. Engaging a furnished room run by an unappealing creature named Mrs. Purdy, he asks the housekeeper the same question he has asked a thousand others; she replies that she has not rented to anyone fitting the lost young woman's description. The despairing man, dejected after five fruitless months of searching, sinks into a chair in his room but is suddenly engulfed by a fragrance he recognizes as hers: mignonette. After frantically but vainly searching the room for some clue of her presence, he rushes back to the landlady, but she insists that she has seen no such woman, who is easily recognizable by a dark mole near her left eyebrow. The young man returns to his room; the odor has vanished, and with it all his hope. He stuffs the cracks of the doors and windows, turns on the gas, and lies down upon the bed. The final scene twists this pathos into sheer irony:

It was Mrs. McCool's night to go with the can for beer. So she fetched it and sat with Mrs. Purdy in one of those subterranean retreats where housekeepers foregather and the worm dieth seldom.

"I rented out my third-floor-back this evening," said Mrs. Purdy, across a fine circle of foam. "A young man took it. He went up to bed two hours ago."

"Now, did ye, Mrs. Purdy, ma'am?" said Mrs. McCool, with intense admiration. "You do be a wonder for rentin' rooms of that kind. And did ye tell him, then?" she concluded in a husky whisper laden with mystery.

"Rooms," said Mrs. Purdy, in her furriest tones, "are furnished for to rent. I did not tell him, Mrs. McCool."

"'Tis right ye are ma'am; 'tis by renting rooms we kape alive. Ye have the rale sense for business, ma'am. There be many people will rayjict the rentin' of a room if they be tould a suicide has been after dyin' in the bed of it."

"As you say, we has our living to be making," remarked Mrs. Purdy.

"Yis, ma'am; 'tis true. 'Tis just one wake ago this day I helped ye lay out the third-floor-back. A pretty slip of a colleen she was to be killin' herself wid the gas—a swate little face she had, Mrs. Purdy, ma'am."

"She'd a-been called handsome, as you say," said Mrs. Purdy, assenting but critical, "but for that mole she had a-growin' by her left eyebrow. Do fill up your glass again, Mrs. McCool." (103)

At first, this story follows the structural pattern of the crossed-paths plot: the initial encounter and divergence are implied, though not so clearly delineated as in "Tobin's Palm" and "Springtime A La Carte," a cloudiness which deepens the mystery and accentuates the sombre atmosphere. However, a promised reunion is neither mentioned nor implied. Whether the man had told the woman he would come but became lost in the big city (as other characters do), or whether he had promised to return and never did, is unknown. All we know is that she disappeared from home; any conclusions must be speculative. Thus, while the young man's course of action is clearly the characteristic pursuit of his lost lover, her course of action is not clear, nor can it be presumed, as in "Tobin's Palm."

Nevertheless, he *is* attempting a reunion, and the city is, again, the obstacle. The young man realizes the futility of searching for a struggling young singer in New York: "He was sure that since her disappearance from home this great, water-girt, city held her somewhere, but it was like a monstrous quicksand shifting its particles constantly, with no foundation, its upper granules of today buried to-morrow in ooze and slime" (100).

The final encounter, the actual crossing of paths, occurs when the young man smells her mignonette and senses her presence. This is the climax of the story and the heart of the surprise, though the reader cannot yet be certain that the roads have indeed crossed. The supernatural dimension of this crossing, combined with the young man's desperate and pathetic certainty, create a powerful scene rarely found in Porter's stories. Finally, the crossing of paths is revealed—or confirmed—in the mildly anticlimactic scene between Mrs. Purdy and her neighbor, providing the final, ironical effect. This post-facto revelation resembles the cross-purposes plot pattern, in which the final convergence unveils a previous encounter.

But again, this ending is not a complete surprise to the astute reader. The odor of the mignonette is the most powerful clue and is consistent with the story's eerie mystery. The housekeeper herself supplies another clue: with her furry voice and unwholesome character—like a "surfeited worm that had eaten its nut to a hollow shell and now sought to fill the vacancy with edible lodgers" (99)—she is hardly reliable, as Blanche Williams points out:

> The shock of this ending is dependent on Mrs. Purdy's lie.... The personality of the woman is such that one may suspect her of lying, even before the act; the suggestion in the frangrance of mignonette confirms the suspicion that Eloise Vashner has occupied the third floor back. It is also true that by keeping the spotlight on the young man—until the final shift—the author makes easier the working of the deceit.[6]

Thus, like the cross-purposes pattern, the crossed-paths pattern is characterized by a specific structural development upon which a number of variations can be worked: the initial encounter which occurs prior to the beginning of the story; the divergence of paths from that union, also occurring in the past, along with the promise of reunion; the attempted meeting which is thwarted by some greater force, usually the Big City, at which point the story generally opens; and finally the reunion itself, the crossing of paths, triggered by some element or movement of fate which may or may not be known prior to the surprise ending. This final crossroads is the crucial point in both the cross-purposes and crossed-paths patterns, but whereas the surprise ending in the first pattern reveals a previous encounter and a conflict of actions, in the latter pattern it reveals no such conflict but rather focuses on the union itself or on the element that triggered the union, marking the culmination of a search for the lost lover.

The third and final route of traversal in the cross pattern is the cross-identity pattern, the one employed most frequently in Porter's New York stories. Whereas the cross-purposes and the crossed-paths patterns both point towards a final, usually physical encounter between *two* characters, the cross-identity pattern hinges upon a psychological encounter within *one* character: that is, the crossroads marks the merging of a character's assumed identity with his true one, hitherto concealed. This concealment can be both physical—which is usually conscious—and psychological—which is usually unconscious. Physical identity here refers specifically to outward appearance, clothes, and apparent social standing; a character concealing a true physical identity consciously masquerades as something he or she is not: i.e., a shopgirl or clerk parades as a wealthy socialite, or a millionaire's son pretends to be a common, humble laborer. The purpose of this role reversal is usually just to see "how the other half lives." Psychological identity, on the other hand, involves an aspect of personality which the character is unaware of until some unexpected event triggers its revelation. What is significant, and what underlies the irony, is the character's certainty that he would react totally opposite to the way he actually does in a given situation.

The characters in the stories can be either on parallel courses or on opposite courses. That is, both may be working class individuals masquerading similarly as rich patrons, or the real identity of one may turn out to be identical to the assumed identity of the other, and vice versa. Either way, the key element is the hidden identity, physical or psychological, and its discovery constitutes the surprise element.

Two typical examples illustrate the physical aspect of the cross-identity pattern: "While the Auto Waits" (really more of an incident than a story) and "Transients in Arcadia." Both follow the general pattern of development characterizing the cross-identity plot: the introduction of two characters, individually and separately; the meeting and interaction of the two; and the revelation of the true identity of the characters, which may be witnessed by one or both of the characters.

The situation of the first tale is this: to a small park at twilight each day comes a young girl dressed in gray, where she sits on a bench and peruses a book. A young man hovers nearby, waiting for a chance to talk with her, a hope which is fulfilled when she drops her book. The ensuing conversation reveals that she is a wealthy lady, grown weary of the endless rounds of clubs, theatres, balls, and other upper class diversions; he is a commoner employed as a cashier in the restaurant facing them across the park. When she rises to leave, indicating that a chauffeured white car is waiting for her nearby, she insists that the young man not accompany her and that he remain on the bench for ten minutes, so as not to see the monogram on the limousine and learn her identity. She moves away swiftly; the young man silently follows her. She passes the waiting limousine, enters the restaurant across the street, and assumes her position at the cash register, visible through the window. The young man strolls slowly back, climbs into the waiting auto, and says, "Club, Henri" (1282).

This situation illustrates the conscious physical reversal of the cross-identity pattern. Two characters, one apparently wealthy, the other apparently poor but respectable, meet and converse, with the conversation being the pivotal point. When they part, the girl leaves by the path of identity along which the young man had apparently come, while the young man takes the path by which the girl had approached. Each thus reveals an identity opposite to the assumed one—and further, the false identity of one matches the true identity of another, so there is a double irony here.

Again, this pattern can be illustrated by a geometric design, where X marks the meeting and conversation of the two characters. A is the path by which the woman has arrived, and B the one by which the man has arrived. Normally, each would continue straight through, remaining on the same paths, but instead, each turns abruptly from his or her respective path, ironically ending up on the exact path by which the other has come. Thus the woman, approaching by path A as a lady of means, retreats by path B' back to her drab life as a cashier, taking over the path which originally belonged to the man. He, in turn, approaching by path B, abruptly turns onto her path, designated by A', and returns to his world of chauffeurs and clubs. The intersection, or cross, marks the spot where conflicting identities meet. But whereas in the other cross plot patterns this crossroads marked a union, in this pattern it witnesses a change: each character exchanges the assumed identity for the real identity, producing the story's twist.[7]

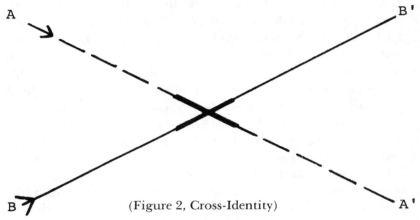

(Figure 2, Cross-Identity)

A similar pattern evolves in "Transients in Arcadia." The setting is a Broadway hotel which is an "oasis in the July desert of Manhattan" (1329), a luxurious hideaway of the wealthy. Into this hotel comes a woman named Mme. Heloise D'Arcy Beaumont, an elite, gracious lady whom the guests immediately love. She emanates the aura of a queen, displaying her glory at dinnertime in a beautiful and stunning gown. A few days later an equally graceful young man, Harold Farrington, registers in the hotel, inquiring about European steamship schedules. The two meet and exchange amenities and aristocratic trivia.

On the last night of the week they dine together, and Mme. Beaumont, wearing the same striking gown, reveals to Mr. Farrington that she is not sailing the next day as she had told him; rather, she is returning to her $8-a-week job as a salesgirl as Casey's Mammoth Store, since her vacation is over. She had saved for a year to spend a week "like a lady" (1332), buying the dress on a dollar-a-week installment plan from O'Dowd & Levinsky.

Whereupon Mr. Farrington reveals that he is actually a collector for O'Dowd & Levinsky and had also saved money for the same purpose as she. They make a date to go to Coney Island together the following weekend.

The same pattern of reversal is evident here as in "While the Auto Waits." Character A enters the picture as a wealthy society woman; character B enters as a young man of leisure and means. They meet and converse, and at the final encounter their true identities are revealed to be opposite to appearance, though in this case the assumed identity does not match the other's true identity. The crossroads with its surprise twist is the point where the assumed identity and the true identity of each character meet; furthermore, the real identity of each character also meets the real identity of the other character, so it is a four-way intersection.

As in the cross-purposes and the crossed-paths patterns, the intersection is significant, and crucial to the surprise ending. But this pattern differs from the other two in having no previous encounter, no divergence, and no mutual dilemma. The final encounter of cross-identity is due merely to chance; no motivation prompts it.

On the other hand, considering just the individual characters and their double identities, this plot pattern is identical to the cross-purposes and crossed-paths patterns. A previous union is apparent, for at some point the two identities—real and assumed—must have been united in the individual character. The point of divergence is also clear: the character has separated his or her identity for a specific purpose (revealed at the cross) and for a temporary period, with the ultimate reunion inherent and inevitable, since the assumed identity must yield to the demands of real identity—a return to a job or simply to a way of life.

In the physical cross-identity pattern, then, it is the dual psychological element of the internal split which is significant. The pattern of this split and reunion is similar to the first two plot patterns, yet the psychological element also clearly distinguishes it from the cross-purposes and the crossed-paths plot patterns. This pattern is further distinguished by the duality of the final encounter, which involves not only the meeting of two identities within one consciousness but also the meeting of two characters within whom such a split has occurred. The meeting itself is incidental and coincidental, although three points about it are important. First, it is significant that both characters have been following parallel courses of action (a characteristic of the cross formula); second, the dual courses set up the double twist at the crossroads; third, some element or elements of coincidence do link these two characters at the crossroads. In "While the Auto Waits," they are the cashier job and the auto itself; in "Transients in Arcadia," the element is Mr. Farrington's job as collector for the very store to which Mme. Beaumont owes money, a coincidence which is consummated when she gives him her last dollar as a first payment and he gives her a receipt.

The physical cross-identity pattern, then, manifested through character appearance, involves a psychological aspect as well.

The psychological pattern, which also culminates in the revelation of some unknown aspect of identity, is illustrated by the story "Proof of the Pudding," again involving two characters who make mutual discoveries. Editor Westbrook of *Minerva* magazine has certain ideas about what constitutes good fiction; Shackleford Dawe, a fiction writer and one of Westbrook's old acquaintances, has equally certain ideas which happen to conflict with Westbrook's. Dawe, once financially comfortable but now destitute through some quirk of fate, is trying unsuccessfully to earn a living writing fiction. When he corners the editor in the park one day, demanding to know why his stories are being rejected by the magazine, Westbrook explains that the climactic language must be effusive and highly colored, arguing that in real life dramatic situations, people would indeed respond with such phrases as, "May high heaven witness that I will rest neither night nor day till the heartless villain that has stolen me child feels the weight of a mother's vengeance!" (1600) Dawe considers such language absurd and unrealistic, and refuses to put it in his stories.

To determine whose theory of realism is correct, Dawe proposes a plan: they will go to his flat and leave a note for his wife saying he has left her for one who "understands the needs of my artistic soul as she never did" (1603). Her reaction will prove whose theory is correct. But upon arriving, they discover a note from Dawe's wife informing him that *she* has left, to join a travelling opera company, adding that Mrs. Westbrook is accompanying her, having grown tired of living with "a combination phonograph, iceberg and dictionary" (1604). The reactions of the two men constitute the conclusion of the story:

> Dawe dropped the letter, covered his face with his trembling hands, and cried out in a deep, vibrating voice:
>
> "My God, why hast thou given me this cup to drink? Since she is false, then let Thy Heaven's fairest gifts, faith and love, become the jesting bywords of traitors and fiends!"
>
> Editor Westbrook's glasses fell to the floor. The fingers of one hand fumbled with a button on his coat as he blurted between his pale lips:
>
> "Say, Shack, ain't that a hell of a note? Wouldn't that knock you off your perch, Shack? Ain't it hell, now, Shack—ain't it?" (1604)

This story, like the previous two, involves a dual interaction: the psychological interaction between one character's two identities, and the physical interaction between two separate characters. But whereas the physical cross-identity pattern hinges upon a merging of identities consciously separated, the surprise here turns on the emergence of an unknown and unsuspected identity. The cross is the point at which each character uncovers an identity opposite to his known identity, but identical to the other character's. So there is both a divergence and a merging: a divergence within the individual and a merging of the two separate characters. This pattern, virtually identical to "While the Auto Waits," can be illustrated with the same diagram:

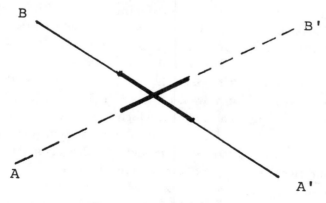

(Figure 3, Cross-Identity)

Here X marks the cross at which the twist occurs. A is the path along which Westbrook is traveling, with B' as the natural continuation of that path. Instead, when he reaches the crossroads, he ironically veers to path A', which is his unknown identity. The same principle guides Dawe, who is traveling by path B, to swerve to B' rather than A', the path he would have followed according to his argument. The further irony, and the double twist, is that each character ends up on the path traveled by the other character, which each had previously scorned.

What distinguishes this pattern from physical cross-identity is the discovery by each character of some quality about himself, particularly ironic because it is directly opposite to what he had always expected to find.

The psychological plot follows the same basic pattern of development as the physical in the introduction of characters, the meeting, and the interaction. But between this point and the surprise twist emerges the conflict (different ideas) and the incident triggering the final reversal, the ironic revelation of characters which distinguishes this pattern. The cross pattern, then, consists of any of a series of sub-patterns by which a story moves towards a final intersection, or crossroads, which marks the moment of surprise. This sudden twist, which forms the heart of the cross pattern, depends upon the meeting of paths to materialize. The plot "possesses its value in the denouement that comes about after a peculiar cross between the two lines of interest."[8]

That denouement involves a reversal, and it is the reversal which provides the shock, the surprise twist, of the story. In the cross-purposes pattern, the reversal links the actions of two characters: each one's action has reversed the effect of the other's. Reversal also characterizes plot movement, since the focus suddenly shifts to a previous time, to an incident which has already occurred but is only now revealed. This reversal of plot movement occurs in the crossed-paths pattern also; in addition; there is a reversal in the character's luck as he discovers, knowingly or unknowingly, the person he seeks. In the cross-identity pattern, of course, the reversal occurs within each character and between the characters, as they exchange identities both internally and externally.

This principle of reversal is similar to one Foster Harris suggests, calling the central point (the X in the earlier diagrams) the "vanishing point," the point at which inner and outer reality merge, which he identifies as the heart of the plot, "the point of reversal, the great secret."[9] Harris, too, designs this principle in geometric fashion:

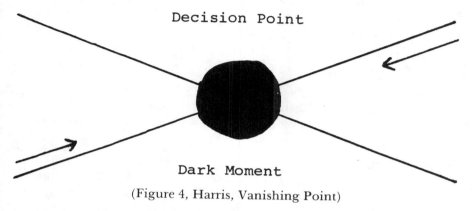

Decision Point

Dark Moment

(Figure 4, Harris, Vanishing Point)

To traverse the dark moment, Harris explains, the character can either hug the right or go straight through:

And here the "twist" you have heard so much about in stories and plotting operates. What logically and intellectually should have been the left hand side of the road suddenly becomes the right. Where you were going, in a twinkling you are coming. You have made a reversal and now that you are through with it you can see that it makes sense on the other side also, but in a reverse order.[10]

The underlying elements of the cross pattern, duality and reversal, take different shapes according to the specific pattern in which they are employed. The three basic cross patterns—cross-purposes, crossed-paths, and cross-identity—overlap and duplicate one another in several respects, yet each possesses a singularly distinctive characteristic. In the cross-purposes pattern, that characteristic is the revelation of a conflicting solution and a previous encounter unknown until the final crossing of paths. In the crossed paths pattern, it is the element of divergence and final reunion; and in the cross-identity pattern, it is the revelation of a hitherto concealed true identity. The three basic patterns and their numerous variations all lead to one common destination: a final crossroads wherein lies the peculiar twist that gives to these stories their distinctive singularity of form.

II

A second structural pattern which recurs in Porter's stories is the triangular plot pattern. The framework of this pattern is just what its name implies: a triangle. A story of this kind involves three main characters whose interaction determines the movement of the story. If we call these characters A, B, and C, then the story can be roughly divided into three segments. In the first, A and B are introduced, and their relationship is established and illustrated, forming a complete scene. In the second segment, character B comes into contact with C, and a similar sequence occurs; the characters interact in some way, in a scene which bears no apparent connection to the preceding one but which turns out to be the crucial link in the triangular arrangement. The third segment completes the triangle, bringing the plot to the culminating point where the surprise ending lies. In this segment, character C interacts with character A in a relationship which may be actual or implied, or even metaphorical. Regardless of its nature, this relationship is vital to the unity and completion of the story. The exposure of this A-C relationship pulls the entire picture into focus, showing that what were seemingly disparate episodes are instead vitally interconnected.

Geometrically, this pattern can obviously be designed as a triangle. Here the three sides A, B, and C represent the individual movement of each character; the numbers 1, 2, 3, and 4 mark the points at which each pair of characters interacts. Point 1, where the story starts, is also point 4, where it ends, so the character who instigates the action is also crucial to its conclusion. In its external structure, this pattern reflects the internal plot, the movement of the characters, the very heart of the story. Just as the three sides of the triangle are independent of one another yet connected, so are the three paths of the characters independent, except when they cross another character's path (again the use of the intersection element so popular with Porter). In most cases, though not always, the characters are unaware of relationships between the other characters.

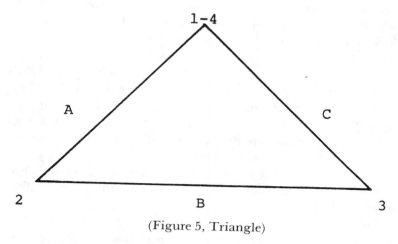

(Figure 5, Triangle)

Three stories will serve to illustrate this triangular pattern. Besides following the basic structural design, they incorporate individual variations, which themselves are integral elements.

The triangular pattern is most obvious in "The Social Triangle," since the story is literally divided into three sections emphasizing the separation of character relationships and doubling the irony at the end. Unlike many of Porter's stories, and despite the relationship which the word "triangle" connotes, "The Social Triangle" is not a love story but rather a tale of idealism. The first character to appear is Ikey Snigglefritz, a tailor's apprentice who, when his long day is finished, "hitched his wagon to such stars as his firmament let shine" (1420). With his twelve-dollar wages on Saturday night, Ikey heads for the bar which his idol, district leader Billy McMahan, frequents. Ikey is awed by the sight of this man, but with a sudden, courageous impulse, he steps out, shakes his hand, and offers to buy him and his friends a drink. In a moment his twelve dollars is spent, but Ikey is happy: "He had shaken the hand of Billy McMahan" (1421).

The point of view then shifts to Billy McMahan and reveals a similar fantasy. McMahan and his wife are dining in a notable saloon; nearby, alone, sits Cortlandt Van Duyckink, a man worth $80 million, who holds a "sacred seat in the exclusive inner circle of society" (1422). With a sudden, audacious impulse, McMahan walks over to Van Duyckink, holds out his hand, and offers to help the philanthropist carry out some planned reforms in McMahan's district. Van Duyckink rises and thanks him, and McMahan, tingling from the attention, returns happily to his seat, for "He had shaken the hand of Cortlandt Van Duyckink" (1423).

The third section of the story then shifts to Van Duyckink's point of view, as he is driving his flashy gray auto through the lower East Side, surveying poverty and planning his reforms. At one point, he alights to examine the structure, and a young man "who seemed to epitomize its degradation, squalor and infelicity" comes down the steps. On a sudden impulse, Van Duyckink grasps his hand and says he is going to help all the people there. Then he drives away, happy, for "He had shaken the hand of Ikey Snigglefritz" (1432).

In this story, which reflects the disparity and stratification of social classes, the initial movement—that is, side A of the triangle, beginning at point 1—centers on Ikey Snigglefritz and his relationship with Billy McMahan, highlighted by an encounter which is pre-planned to some extent but which materializes through a sudden "audacious" impulse. The segment concludes when Ikey leaves, broke but content. The continuation of the movement in the second segment, centering on Billy McMahan, his thoughts and feelings, is highlighted by his meeting—accidental and again impulsive—with Cortlandt Van Duyckink, and culminates in the same feeling of satisfaction. The final segment, focusing on the actions of Van Duyckink, carries the plot development back to the starting point, climaxing in the encounter between Van Duyckink and Snigglefritz, a meeting which concludes the story not in a denouement of action nor even a sudden turn of events, but rather on a small irony of human existence, a reworking of the old "small world" saying.

The structural pattern of the plot also reflects the movement of the characters. Just as each side of the triangle proceeds towards an intersection, so does the path of each character move toward a meeting with another character, a meeting which is the high point of each one's life. The intersection is a point, a goal for which each one is striving, a fulfillment of hopes and ideals. The intersection marks a point at which each character achieves some personal satisfaction of the sort which would, to most people, probably seem inappropriate for persons of their position.

The plot proceeds in a movement from lower to upper class, just as the characters reach upwards for some star that is above them. The final culminating point occurs where the highest level touches the lowest: Van Duyckink meets Ikey. Technically, this meeting is ironic because of the previous encounters in the story. In a human sense, though, it is not ironic in the least: if all men, regardless of social position, dream the same dreams and strive for similar high ideals, such a meeting is perfectly logical and right.

The similarity of ideals is the unifying element of the story and of the triangular pattern, and Porter emphasizes this interrelationship by repeating words and phrases in each succeeding situation. Consider, for example, the three moments at which the characters step forward to grasp their ideals:

> And there was born suddenly in the worshipful soul of Ikey an audacious, thrilling impulse.
> He stepped forward into the little cleared space in which his majesty moved, and held out his hand. (1420)
> And then Billy McMahan conceived and accomplished the most startling and audacious act of his life. He rose deliberately and walked over to Cortlandt Van Duyckink's table and held out his hand. (1422)
> Obeying a sudden impulse, Van Duyckink stepped out and warmly grasped the hand of what seemed to him a living rebuke. (1423)

Ikey and McMahan's movements are virtually identical: both are couched in the metaphor of birth, both involve decision and movement, both use the word "audacious," and in the same phrase. Van Duyckink's movement is similar also, although detached by a varied wording; but then, Van Duyckink himself was quite detached in his life from such people.

The endings of the segments, the denouement of each character's encounter, are even more striking in their similarity. Compare:

> Ikey remained in his ecstatic trance of joy.... He had shaken the hand of Billy McMahan. (1421)
> Billy McMahan was happy.
> He had shaken the hand of Cortlandt Van Duyckink. (1423)
> He was near to being a happy man.
> He had shaken the hand of Ikey Snigglefritz. (1423)

Socially, these characters are worlds apart; only peripherally do they come in contact with one another, even if physically. But spiritually, ideally, in the realm of goals and ambitions, they are all seekers of a dream: "For each of us, when our day's work is done, must seek our ideal, whether it be love or pinochle or lobster á la Newburg, or the sweet silence of the musty bookshelves" (1420).

A story which does incorporate the triangle pattern in its traditional love context is "Roses, Ruses and Romance," involving two men and a woman. The story opens as a young writer named Ravenel is lamenting to his friend Sammy Brown the death of Romance, judging by the latest literary fare in magazines. Sammy, a broker, comes to Ravenel's apartment several times a week to sit in the leather armchair by the window. On this day, Ravenel reads a poem of his which the magazine has published, entitled "The Four Roses"; Sammy then leaves to keep an engagement. The next afternoon, as Ravenel is working on his poems, he is suddenly enthralled by the white-clad vision of a beautiful woman in the old mansion opposite his window. Romance had risen again. Later that afternoon, he looks out across the garden again and sees in the window four small vases, each containing a full-blown rose. He decides she must have read his poem and is responding by means of Romance. Then he spies a small flower pot beside the roses, identifying its plant as a nutmeg geranium, which means (as he discovers in a book of "useless information") "I expect a meeting" (1315). As Ravenel is contriving how to arrange this meeting, Sammy enters in all his ultra-modernity and assumes his seat by the window. After glancing out, he rises hastily, proclaiming an appointment in ten minutes. When Ravenel inquires why he even came if he had a previous engagement, Sammy falters at first, then admits that he is engaged to a woman in the house next door, but since her father resists the marriage and keeps a close eye on her, she and Sammy must arrange meetings secretly. The outcome from this point is easy to predict: Ravenel asks Sammy how he gets his tip, and the friend replies that the four roses mean four o'clock. " 'But the geranium?' persists Ravenel, clutching at the end of flying Romance's trailing robe. 'Means half-past,' shouted Sammy from the hall. 'See you tomorrow' " (1316).

In this story, the first segment focuses on the relationship between Ravenel and Sammy, inconspicuously planting the clues upon which the final irony is based and ending with the separation of the two characters. The second segment, focusing on Ravenel alone in his apartment, introduces the relationship between him and character C, a relationship which is abstract, involving no physical contact except a glance across the garden, and evolved completely in the romantic imagination of Ravenel; the segment ends with Sammy's entrance. The third segment again involves Ravenel and Sammy, culminating in the revelation of the relationship between Sammy and Edith—characters A and C. This relationship is oblique also, the actual physical meeting occurring outside the direct action of the story.

Thus, the story presents first the relationship between Ravenel and Sammy, then the romantic but imaginary relationship between the woman and Ravenel, and finally the relationship between Sammy and Edith, which already existed, but unknown to either the reader or Ravenel. Unlike "The Social Triangle," the initial point (1) of this story involves two characters, so there are necessarily three characters rather than two at the culminating point (4), a variation which only serves to reinforce the triangular nature of the plot and the action. Again, the unity and coherence of the story depend upon the elucidation of this third and final relationship, thus completing the triangle.

This story depends more on the typical surprise twist than does "The Social Triangle," in which the element of surprise is downplayed, subordinate to the deeper, more significant irony of human interaction. "Roses, Ruses and Romance" makes use of the element so common to the cross patterns: the revelation of a preexisting relationship. But here it does not occur in the wake of a twist; rather, it is the focus of the final portion of the story, providing the point of irony which ties together all the parts. The revelation of this relationship makes clear why Sammy liked to sit in the chair by Ravenel's window, why the young woman placed the roses in the window, and why Sammy had to leave so abruptly, and it connects the otherwise unrelated events of segments one and two.

But there is a second, almost allegorical movement in the story, involving the relationship between Ravenel and Romance; though it is not triangular, it is nevertheless necessary to the story's irony, infusing a deeper, more meaningful twist than the superficial one of the interfering lover.

At the outset of the story, Ravenel is complaining that "Romance is dead" (1312), reciting the dull, mechanical, unimaginative contents of a magazine "that once printed Poe and Lowell and Whitman and Bret Harte and DuMaurier and Lanier" (1312), calling all of it "an obituary on Romance" (1312). Sammy Brown, on the other hand, "had no tears for departed Romance" (1313).

The next day, as Ravenel is working on his poetry, Romance is reborn in the appearance of the woman, "the angel of all his dreams of romance and poesy" (1314). A romantic haze descends upon the cold reality Ravenal feared had taken hold; his vision seems "to challenge the poet's flaunt at romance and to punish him for his recreancy to the undying spirit of youth and beauty" (1314). She, in the placement of the emblematic roses, consummates his romantic illusion by unknowingly entering into it with him.

But following this wondrous resurrection, Romance returns to its grave with the intrusion of the "perfect embodiment of modernity and the day's sordid practicality" (1313), Sammy Brown. The irony is doubled: the puncturing of Ravenel's romantic bubble, and the fact that it is Sammy, shunner of Romance, who is the intended recipient of the rose message.

This stream of Romance flows beneath the triangular surface of the story: in segment one Romance is purportedly dead; in segment two, it surges into life and flourishes, both for Ravenel and for the story, since the scene would otherwise hold no meaning; in segment three, Romance retreats, dies back down, ending up at the same point where it was at the beginning of the story. Thus, the concept of Romance is essential to the development of the story, logically reinforcing the triangular nature of the plot.

"Roses, Ruses and Romance," then, is structured on the pattern of the triangular plot—even the title is three-cornered. It moves from the relationship between A and B, to that between B and C, and finally to the one between A and C, with the relationships between A and B, and B and C also involved. The triangular pattern of this plot is reinforced by the nature of the story, founded on the proverbial love triangle. Further reinforcing this theme and simultaneously acting on the structural movement of the plot is the concept of Romance, which provides the impetus for development and which assumes the same form at the beginning and ending points of the triangle.

A final illustration of the triangular pattern is one of Porter's most tender stories, "The Last Leaf," which is based neither on social nor romantic relationships but rather on artistic ones, although like "The Social Triangle," the story involves the pursuit of dreams, and like "Roses, Ruses and Romance," the final relationship is a metaphorical one.

The story centers on two young artists, Sue and Johnsy (Joanne), living in a third floor studio of a squatty brick house in Greenwich Village. In November, when pneumonia is widespread, Johnsy falls victim to it and lies in her bed, staring at the blank face of the brick house next door, completely resigned to her fate. The doctor tells Sue that the patient's only chance to recover—about one in ten—hinges on her determination to get well. Sue maintains a cheerful countenance around the sick girl, but instead of responding, Johnsy counts the remaining leaves on the ivy vine by the brick wall as they are blown off by the winter wind. "When the last one falls, I must go, too," she whispers (1457). Sue chides her for such foolishness, then goes downstairs to ask an aging German artist named Behrman to model for her. Behrman, past sixty, is an indefatigable artist who has never found success but who "still talked about his coming masterpiece" (1457). When Sue tells him of Johnsy's fatal fantasy, he scoffs in disgust, then agrees to model for her.

The next morning, when Sue awakens, Johnsy orders the shade raised, but despite a raging storm the night past, one leaf still clings tenaciously to the vine. It hangs there all day, and on through the night and another fierce storm. When, by the next morning, it has still not fallen, Johnsy regains strength, realizing her own foolishness. When the doctor comes that afternoon he reports her chances increased to 50-50, adding that he must tend to another case, old Behrman downstairs. By the next day, Johnsy is out of danger; in the afternoon, Sue comes to the bed where her friend sits knitting:

"I have something to tell you, white mouse," she said. "Mr. Behrman died of pneumonia to-day in the hospital. He was ill only two days. The janitor found him on the morning of the first day in his room downstairs helpless with pain. His shoes and clothing were wet through and icy cold. They couldn't imagine where he had been on such a dreadful night. And then they found a lantern, still lighted, and a ladder that had been dragged from its place and some scattered brushes, and a palette with green and yellow colors mixed on it, and—look out the window, dear, at the last ivy leaf on the wall. Didn't you wonder why it never fluttered or moved when the wind blew? Ah, darling, it's Behrman's masterpiece—he painted it there the night that the last leaf fell." (1459)

The initial segment (side A) of this story presents the situation of and relationship between the first two characters (A and B), Sue and Johnsy. While it includes some exposition, the segment focuses on the scene where Johnsy acknowledges to Sue her acceptance of imminent death. At point 2 on the triangle, Sue leaves Johnsy and segment two begins (side B). This portion involves the interaction between characters B and C, Sue and old Behrman, a "fierce little old man, who scoffed terribly at softness in anyone, and who regarded himself as especial mastiff-in-waiting to protect the two young artists in the studio above" (1457). Here Sue reveals to Behrman Johnsy's fantasy of dying with the last leaf.

The third segment, like that of "Roses, Ruses and Romance," involves characters A and B, but is based on the relationship between A and C, which is not revealed until the last sentence. It is even more metaphorical than in the previous story, for no physical interaction is indicated. Rather, it is wholly spiritual, symbolized by the leaf which Behrman paints upon the wall to keep Johnsy alive; it is as crucial to the story as it is to Johnsy's recovery, resulting ironically in Behrman's fatal illness, Johnsy's recovery, and the old man's fulfillment of his dream to paint a masterpiece.

Besides guiding the plot movement, a triangular pattern defines the relationships as well. In segment one (A) we have Johnsy's relationship to death and to Sue; in B there is the relationship between Sue and Behrman, Behrman and the girls (protective), and Behrman and the human spirit; in C it is Johnsy and Sue again, Johnsy and Behrman, Behrman and art, and finally, Behrman and death. Several connections can be drawn here, but one example will suffice: Johnsy's response to death (A) leads directly to Sue's conversation with Behrman (B) which in turn prompts Behrman's action (C) leading to his death, which connects him back to Johnsy. The relationships among these three characters involve protective instincts, physical intervention, and a spiritual, even existential dimension whereby they contribute purpose to each others' lives.

Thus, Porter's triangular plot pattern moves through three segments and involves the interrelationship of three characters, with the unity of the story depending upon the final connection between characters A and C. Like the cross pattern, this one incorporates the element of intersection, but this time there are three such crossings, with the final one making clear the significance of the first two. The pattern reflects the movement of the plot and the relationships of the characters, and this interplay strengthens the stories themselves and validates the plot pattern and Porter's artistic ability. Since the triangle so often symbolizes human relationships and existential mysteries, the pattern seems appropriate for Porter's stories about the beauty, sadness, and irony of human involvements.

III

Habit is one of the themes that most appealed to Porter's narrative instincts. Referring to the author's conviction about habit his biographer writes, "It is that when the old environment comes back the old habit is pretty sure to come with it."[11] This sure belief in the power of recurrence emerges in several stories which show the dull, daily routines of ordinary people suddenly and unexpectedly disrupted. The pattern of these stories, which may be called the habit pattern, generally proceeds in a circular movement, being thrown off track by some unforeseen occurrence but finally ending up right back where it began.

The story based upon the habit pattern usually involves a husband and wife locked into the drab, predictable rut of domestic life. The opening of the story chronicles this monotonous existence and establishes the routine on which the variation will occur. Into this stifling world some occurrence intrudes, causing chaos to which characters react in various ways. The source of the disruption may range from an everyday crisis to a fantastic call of adventure that only the Big City can provide. Following the development and resolution of this intrusion, the character or characters return to their routine existence, usually resuming exactly where they had left off, down to the very word or movement, as though a movie, frozen on one frame, begins rolling again.

The most exemplary story based on the habit pattern, appropriately titled "The Pendulum," is the story often cited by those who discuss Porter's fascination with habit. As its title suggests, "The Pendulum" deals with the predictable regularity of one man's domestic lifestyle and the psychological upheaval rendered by a brief interruption of that cycle.

On a day just like all others, John Perkins is drifting homeward after work, mulling gloomily over the monotony of the evening ahead, for no surprises await "a man who has been married two years and lives in a flat" (1383). His wife Katy will greet him at the door; he will read the evening paper; they will eat dinner listening to the sounds of the evening routines beginning in Frogmore flats. Then at 8:15 Perkins will reach for his hat, whereupon Katy will demand, "Now where are you going, I'd like to know, John Perkins?" And Perkins will reply, clocklike, "Thought I'd drop up to McCloskey's,...and play a game or two of pool with the fellows" (1384).

But when Perkins arrives at home, this gloomy vision evaporates, for the apartment is in disarray and there is no Katy to greet him, only a note dangling from the gas jet telling him that her mother has suddenly been taken ill. Bewildered and lost by the unexpected change—for it is "a break in a routine that had never varied, and it left him dazed" (1385)—Perkins sits alone in the flat, sadly perceiving the pleasure and comfort of the shattered lifestyle that only a short while ago had been the cause of his depression and gloom. He looks longingly at the lingering traces of Katy's presence, trying to cope with the sudden emptiness. Prompted by these mirages of solitude, Perkins vows that things will be different when she returns; he will neglect her no more and will appreciate her as he ought. At that moment, Katy enters the flat with the news that her mother was not seriously ill after all. Whereupon:

Nobody heard the click and rattle of the cogwheels as the third-floor-front of the Frogmore flats buzzed its machinery back into the Order of Things. A band slipped, a spring was touched, the gear was adjusted and the wheels revolve in their old orbit.

John Perkins looked at the clock. It was 815 [sic]. He reached for his hat and walked to the door.

"Now, where are you going, I'd like to know, John Perkins?" asked Katy, in a querulous tone.

"Thought I'd drop up to McCloskey's," said John, "and play a game or two of pool with the fellows." (1386-87)

The circular pattern which forms the basis of this plot is obviously the domestic routine of Mr. and Mrs. Perkins. This cycle binds the story just as it holds together the lives of its practitioners. The disruptive element—the sudden illness of Katy's mother which precipitates her hasty departure—breaks this routine, leaving Perkins at a loss.

Such a plot structure is intricately intertwined with content. The story depends for unity and completion on a return to the initial situation; without this return, this closing of the circle, the deviation would be meaningless, and the story would have no central purpose. Likewise, John Perkins himself depends on the return to that initial situation. Without this regularity his life loses its meaning and purpose; he, like the story, would be adrift in a void of absurdity.

Paradoxically, the deviation also is necessary to both the story and John Perkins' existence. Without this disruptive element, the story would go nowhere; more accurately, it would revolve in an endless and meaningless circle of habit. It is the intrusion of the conflict, the break in routine, which propels the narrative development, for before the story can return to the starting point, achieving unity, it needs a deviation.

Similarly, John Perkins needs the crucial disturbance to appreciate the security of his habitual routine. In the beginning of the story, he curses the predictability and certainty of his life, but when those elements are removed—as if in response to his lament—he panics in the new realty; when his routine is restored, he falls back into it gratefully, with not a moment to lose.

His personality corresponds to this deviation, for his change of attitude turns out to be as temporary as the respite from routine. In the short but agonizing period that Katy is gone, Perkins vows that the cycle will be broken and that he will cease to neglect her. These promises and good intentions, however, dissolve instantly when she returns.

Habit, then, provides a basis of existence for both the story and John Perkins. The circularity of routine carries the story from its starting point to its conclusion, with the deviation accentuating the theme. Similarly, the circularity of routine carries Perkins through life, providing the security he needs, and the disruption enables him to realize this dependency and welcome its return.

The same pattern of normalcy—disruption—resolution— return to normalcy underlies "Between Rounds," the amusing story of an Irish boarding house couple. In the midst of a typical evening argument in which Mr. and Mrs. McCaskey heave crockery and casseroles at one another, the mistress of the boarding house shrieks, having discovered that her little boy is missing. The McCaskeys cease their duel, come to the window "to recover their second wind" (18), and lament the loss. Caught in sentimentality, they apologize to each other and entwine arms, but when the landlady discovers the boy hidden asleep behind a roll of linoleum the two turn back into the room and resume their battle as before.

Again, the circular basis of the plot is clear: the exchange of dinner dishes opens and closes the action, the frightful disappearance of the boy causes a deviation from this normal routine, and once that problem is resolved, the McCaskeys pick up where they left off. Again, the deviation manifests itself in the characters' personalities, as both Mr. and Mrs. McCaskey apologize to each other for their actions (although there is no resolve never to do it again). The "tragedy" provides a respite from their usual practice of mutual abuse, but once it's resolved, they return unhesitantly to their old habit.

This structure of habit is reinforced by the movements of the other characters as well. For Mrs. Murphy, the disappearance of her child marks a disruption in routine; for Major Grigg, a boarder, it provides an opportunity to slip into town, ostensibly to look for the child, since his wife—who never allows him out after dark— now urges him on. The periodic rounds of Policeman Cleary also emphasize the routine, for the beginning and ending of the story are marked by his passing beneath the McCaskeys' window and hearing the familiar sounds of their domestic discussion.

The plot begins at point A—the quarrel—proceeds through the introduction, development, and resolution of the problem, and returns to point A for its conclusion. As in "The Pendulum," content and form are closely linked: the husband and wife begin at point A, their usual domestic interchange, move to a temporary peace, then return to point A after affairs have returned to normal. Just as in "The Pendulum," habit provides the basis and the unifying element both for the plot action and for the lives of the characters.

A final story illustrating Porter's use of the habit plot pattern is "The Complete Life of John Hopkins," in which the disruptive element is not a typical crisis such as an illness or a lost child, but is rather a twist of fate which triggers an extraordinary adventure that, despite its digression from the ordinary, has no apparent effect whatsoever on the character involved.

Like the preceding two stories, "The Complete Life of John Hopkins" deals with a mundane man who tries to spice up the "tasteless dough of existence" with a few raisins of after-dinner conversation. So he tells his wife about his boss wearing a new spring suit to work: "It's a gray with—" (1258). Suddenly Hopkins is seized with the urge for a cigar and heads out to the corner market where, finding himself without change, he gets into a fight with the storekeeper and sprints from the scene. As he is fleeing, the driver of a red car motions him to jump in, which he does, grateful for the timely escape. The automobile bears him to a brownstone mansion; he is ushered into the presence of a young woman who beseeches his protection. A reader of historical novels, the young lady is apparently caught up in the delusions of chivalry and romance, and requests Hopkins to protect her from a man in the next room. The man, obviously some relative, escorts Hopkins from the house and chides Bess for getting so carried away with her fantasies. As for John Hopkins, he returns to his flat, answers in the affirmative his wife's question about his cigar, then sits down on the sofa and says, " 'I was telling you...about Mr. Whipple's suit. It's a gray, with an invisible check, and it looks fine' " (1261).

The same plot pattern upon which the first two stories are built is evident here. The story opens on the usual routine of two people, then narrows its focus to one character as he takes a routine jaunt for a routine cigar. Even the quarrel with the grocer, while maybe not an everyday occurrence, is not much out of the ordinary for Hopkins. But when the mysterious red car lures him into its depths, Hopkins proceeds on an adventure which is totally removed from his ordinary existence. The woman he encounters is completely opposite to his wife, and the knightly love he feels toward her is also strange and new to him.

The exaggerated world of imaginative romance (perhaps a spoof on the contemporary fictional rage) further emphasizes the transformation of the ordinary. Bess, perturbed by the removal of her dangerous dog, petulantly sends her chauffeur to fetch her cousin, but when the latter cannot be found, the chauffeur recruits Hopkins. During his adventure, however, Hopkins exhibits hardly any changes of personality, and when he is escorted from the house, he makes his way back to his flat, back to the routine he had left, picking up the thread of conversation exactly where he had left it hanging, making not the slightest mention of his interlude. In this ambivalence he is unlike the characters in the other two stories, who exhibit some attitude changes during the deviation period. Aside from the knightly love toward Bess and the chivalric response to her request, Hopkins seems to take the situation in stride as though it were not in the least unusual.

Again, plot structure and content are interrelated. The plot pattern proceeds from a given point and returns to that point by way of a digression necessary to the departure and return. Likewise, Hopkins proceeds from a given point—his flat—back to that same point by way of a rather fantastic adventure. The return to this existence concludes both the story and Hopkins' day, and also provides the story structure with its necessary unifying element.

The pattern of habit, then, is built upon two vying elements: routine, which forms a circular pattern on which the characters' lives and the plot's movement are based, with identical beginning and ending points; and deviation, essential to the development of the plot and crucial to the ultimate contrast which the story makes.

Once again, the pattern can be transformed into a geometric design. The circle, of course, represents the element of routine, and the dotted line the element of deviation. The solidity of the circle is usually more forceful than the temporary deviation, ultimately sucking the character back into its path. Point A marks the opening of the story, where the routine is defined; point B marks the moment of disturbance: John Perkins' arrival at an empty flat, the disappearance of Mrs. Murphy's boy, John Hopkins' encounter with the red car. The path of C is the procedure of events which then ensues, continuing until point D, at which order is restored: Katy returns, Mrs. Murphy's boy is found, John Hopkins comes back to his flat. The characters then return to point A and the cycle begins again—without the deviation, of course.

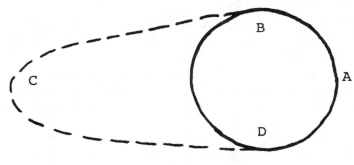

(Figure 6, Habit)

The habit plot, by its nature, revolves around the ironic contrast between ordinary routine and disruptive change. Further irony emerges when a character in such a story, suffering from the ennui of a predictable existence, is distraught when some disaster suddenly frees him from that routine and wishes desperately for its return, a wish that is ultimately (if not predictably) fulfilled.

The ending of a habit story hinges upon the return to the initial routine, the closing of the circle, and the re-affirmation of the power of habit. The deviation is necessary to propel the plot toward this ultimate conclusion, and the surprise—if such a predictable ending can be considered a surprise—lies in the ironic return to such an existence after some unusual digression, as though nothing had ever happened. Such a pattern emphasizes the power of habit, and the strength of human dependence upon it.

IV

A fourth plot pattern which Porter employs frequently in his stories embodies his romantic attitude toward the big city and reflects the spirit of adventure which he acknowledges as the city's essence. This pattern is the quest, so called because its distinctive element is the search. The character in a story built on the quest pattern sets out in search of something; that search constitutes the basic action and development of the story (or in some cases, the episode). The quest is not for something so marvelous as a grail or golden fleece, but it is equally elusive—usually an adventure, an answer to a puzzling question or riddle, or even occasionally a tangible object, such as a peach.

In the course of the quest, the character encounters a number of different people to whom he puts his question, but usually none can provide a satisfactory answer. Having failed in the attempt to learn the answer from someone wiser, and ending back where he began, he then discovers the solution "right in his own back yard": within himself. If it is adventure the character seeks, the pattern is a bit different, since he is not searching for something specific but is ready and waiting for whatever finger of chance might beckon to him.

The quest for the answer to a puzzling question is usually narrated in the first person, as in "The Voice of the City," where the narrator seeks to know what "the voice of agglomerated mankind" (1254) sounds like; to comprehend "the composite vocal message of massed humanity" (1254). In pursuit of an answer, he asks five different people: the lovely Aurelia, who can only smile sweetly and admit that all cities say the same thing; Billy Magnus, the finest bartender around, who is too caught up in the drinking world to even comprehend the question; a cop on the corner, who persuades the narrator to stand in for a moment while he makes a quick nightly rendezvous with his new bride; next the narrator intercepts his poet friend and inquires what the city would say if it should speak, but the poet, hurrying to see some fabled young woman, asks if his tie is straight; finally, cornering a newsboy and fumbling for coins, the narrator asks the question once more, but the boy just says, "Quit yer kiddin' " (1256).

So, having failed in his quest, the narrator returns to the park to sit and meditate:

And then, as swift as light from a fixed star, the answer came to me. I arose and hurried—hurried as so many reasoners must, back around my circle. I knew the answer and I hugged it in my breast as I flew, fearing lest someone would stop me and demand my secret.

Aurelia was still on the stoop. The moon was higher and the ivy shadows were deeper. I sat at her side and we watched a little cloud tilt at the drifting moon. . . .

After half an hour Aurelia said, with that smile of hers:
"Do you know, you haven't spoken a word since you came back!"
"That," said I, nodding wisely, "is the Voice of the City." (1257)

This quest follows the question-answer pattern. The question is born of the narrator's curiosity; unable to supply the answer himself, he sets out to ask others who might know. Their answers, however, are his obstacles: the bartender and the policeman, who interact with the city's inhabitants daily, cannot even understand the question; the poet, whose function is to transform abstract ideas into words, does not even hear the question. Frustrated in his attempt, the narrator "thought and thought, and wondered why none could tell me what I asked for" (1256); then he finds the answer within himself, achieving a sense of peace and satisfaction from the new-found knowledge.

The question-answer content of the plot emphasizes and reinforces the quest pattern, beginning with a question and ending with an answer, with the development also constructed around a series of questions. This structure reflects the nature of the main character involved, who cannot rest until he finds his answer; the end of the quest therefore coincides with the conclusion of the story. This isn't the usual surprise ending; it is more subtle, involving a sudden irony that the answer isn't what was expected. The "voice," as it turns out, isn't a voice at all, for it says nothing.

The quest pattern resembles both the habit and the triangular patterns, in that the character ends up where he began, having achieved nothing but the knowledge that nobody had the answer he sought.

"Man About Town" follows a similar question-answer pattern. This time the character, again a first person narrator, seeks to define not the nature of the city but the nature of a person: specifically, the character type known as the Man About Town. Again, this curiosity takes him on a round of questioning which yields no answer. A newspaper reporter can only define him by negation and a series of added characteristics; a bartender offers an even less satisfactory answer; a Salvation Army solicitor labels him as a wicked type and rattles her money box. Then the narrator questions a critic friend, who in a long and eloquent reply, classifies the type to the narrator's satisfaction, where upon the latter says, "I must meet

one face to face. I must study the Man About Town at first hand"
(36) and leaves to pursue the real person, a quest which is an end
in itself: "The pursuit of my type gave a pleasant savor of life
and interest to the air I breathed. I was glad to be in a city so
great, so complex and diversified" (37). Crossing the street in his
reverie, the narrator is struck by a car, and awakens to find himself
in a hospital bed, under the hand of a nurse and near the grinning
face of a young doctor who hands him a morning newspaper:

"Want to see how it happened?" he asked, cheerily. I read the article.
Its headlines began where I heard the buzzing leave off the night before. It
closed with these lines:
"——Bellevue Hospital, where it was said that his injuries were not serious.
He appeared to be a typical Man about Town." (37)

As before, the narrator poses a question he cannot answer and
seeks the truth among the diverse city types; as before, he ends
up where he began, mulling over the question, although this time
he has managed to discover a partial answer; and again he ultimately
finds the answer within himself, this time even more literally.
Structurally, this story follows the same pattern as "The Voice of
the City," opening with a question, ending with an answer, and
plotted in between with a similar series of questions (to similar
or identical types of people) whose answers pose obstacles of
communication and understanding. Like "The Voice of the City,"
this pattern reflects the character on a search, ending when he finds
that truth.

The catalytic question in both stories springs from the city
itself—a fascination with it and a desire to know it better. In the
first one, the narrator wants to understand the spirit of the
metropolis:

Here are 4,000,000 people,....compressed upon an island.... The conjunction
of so many units into so small a space must result in an identity—or, rather
a homogeneity—that finds its oral expression through a common channel.
It is, as you might say, a consensus of translation, concentrating in a crystallized,
general idea which reveals itself in what may be termed The Voice of the City.
(1254)

The "Man About Town" seeks to understand one of the multifarious forms which embodies the very mystery, diversity, and adventure of the city. If the first character seeks the city in a sound, the second seeks it in a person,

a man who had a hopeless case of the peculiar New York disease of wanting to see and know.... He follows rigidly the conventions of dress and manners; but in the business of poking his nose into places where he does not belong he could give pointers to a civet or a jackdaw.... He is curiosity, impudence. (36)

Sometimes, though, the question is practical—how to dispose of money, for example. In "One Thousand Dollars," young Robert Gillian has inherited a sum of a thousand dollars from his late uncle, and he finds it a "confoundedly awkward amount" of money to deal with: too little to do anything splendid with, but too much to just toss away on tidbits (1285). However, the will stipulates that he report to the executors of the estate on the expenditure of the money.

Thereupon, Gillian asks a number of people just what he can do with one thousand dollars. Old Bryson at the club suggests he buy "Miss Lotta Lauriere a diamond pendant" (1287), so he goes to the theatre where that lady is preparing for a performance. She agrees carelessly to the offer, then adds, "Say, Bobby, did you see that necklace Della Stacey had on the other night? $2200 it cost at Tiffany's" (1287). So Gillian leaves and puts the question to a cabbie, who promptly replies that he would open a saloon. Farther down Broadway, Gillian steps from the cab and asks a blind beggar, who pulls out his bank book and shows Gillian a balance of $1,785. Then Gillian goes to his late uncle's home, where a young ward of the old man, named Miriam Hayden, lives. Gillian is in love with her, but she does not share the feelings. He tells her that the lawyers discovered a postscript to the will, leaving the thousand dollars to her, and after committing his expenditure to paper, he delivers the sealed envelope to the lawyers, who then drag from the safe another sealed envelope, open and read it. This envelope had been left by the uncle with strict instructions that it remain unopened until the one thousand dollars had been accounted for; now the contents reveal that another $50,000 is to be awarded to the nephew if his disposition of the original thousand has been "prudent, wise or unselfish" (1289). If not, then Miss Hayden is to inherit the money.

At this point Gillian grabs the envelope containing his account, tears it to shreds, and informs the lawyers gaily that he had lost the thousand dollars on the races; then, whistling gaily, leaves them to shake their heads sadly.

This story incorporates the typical double twist of the patterns discussed earlier, but the major portion follows the quest pattern. The character involved confronts a dilemma, seeks a solution by questioning a number of people, and then ends up solving it himself anyway. The story would end at this point if it followed the exact pattern of the quest illustrated by the first two stories. It does not, however; a double surprise is yet to come. The first is that Robert is to inherit more money because of his generous treatment of the young lady; the second is that he deliberately disqualifies himself so that Miriam may inherit it, an act which is consistent with his feelings toward her. Thus, his quest ends not only in satisfaction for himself but in happiness for someone else, and again, the same structural and internal connection can be traced.

The quest pattern is a bit different in a story like "The Green Door." The crucial motif of the search is still present, but rather than the answer to a question, the character in this version seeks adventure and mystery. He too sets out purposefully, but rather than proceeding through a series of questions and unsatisfactory answers, he moves through a series of steps, and though unsure where to look, he ultimately finds what he seeks—or it finds him. This adventure is not any marvelous event or experience, however, although stereotypical elements such as the damsel-in-distress might be included. But so deeply is the spirit of adventure rooted within the character that he transforms what might be nonchalant, unremarkable events for a less imaginative soul into harbingers of mystery and secrets to be uncovered. It is this attitude which defines the adventure-seeker in Porter's stories and enables him to discover what he does.

Such a character is Rudolph Steiner of "The Green Door," by day a piano store salesman, but by night a true adventurer "in search of the unexpected and the egregious" (64). One evening, as Rudolph strolls past a dentist's office, a huge Negro distributing cards slips one deftly into Rudolph's unseeking hand. When

Rudolph casually glances down, he is startled to discover that one side is blank while the other contains three words: The Green Door. Other cards, which their recipients are tossing to the ground, are advertisements for dental service. Rudolph circles back by the Negro and receives the same kind of card; but a third time he gets only a cold stare. Curious, searching out the mystery, Rudolph surveys the building which houses the dentist's office, enters, and climbs to the third floor. There, in the dim light of a gas jet, he sees a green door; after only a momentary hesitation, he knocks and is met by a young shopgirl faint with starvation. Struck by her beauty and her pathetic condition, he rushes back out for food to restore her, then leaves with the promise to check on her the next day. As he departs, he discovers that every door in the hallway, and on the floor above to which he ascends, is painted green.

Returning to the sidewalk, he confronts the Negro, demanding to know the meaning of the cards, whereupon the Negro nods to a nearby theatre whose blazing marquee reads "The Green Door."

Just as the narrator with a specific question eventually finds the answer within himself, so the character in this story finds adventure and romance within his own mind. His desire to experience strange wonders and his readiness to accept the incredible sharpen his vision and heighten his senses, transforming the ordinary city streets into places thick with intrigue. It is this spirit which causes Rudolph to read a free theatre ticket as an enigmatic clue and to telescope his sight to only one green door in a hallway filled with them. Adventure is not an entity separate from the individual; rather, it is a state of mind, flowering—at least in Porter's stories—in the individual's union with the city.

As in "The Voice of the City" and "Man About Town," the sprawling metropolis is itself a key ingredient in the action. The city breeds mystery and excitement; it has a voice; it manifests itself in strange, curious characters; in its corners and dark alleys lurk the thrill of the unexpected, the flash of chance, the once-knocking opportunity.

This fusion of the individual with the answer he seeks characterizes the quest pattern. What he seeks, he finds within himself, although he must launch the search before he can learn this simple truth. In "The Green Door," the clarification of the mystery does not lessen its impact, but rather reinforces the idea that it is the character's own attitude and eagerness that lead him to the green door and the starving but lovely young girl. It is not so much a matter of waiting for adventure to cross one's path as it is of transforming life into adventure.

The quest pattern, then, consists of three main parts: the presentation or introduction of the problem, the search for a solution or answer, and the ultimate discovery of the answer within one's self. If the problem takes the form of a specific question, the character proceeds through a series of question-answer rounds with several people who cannot tell him what he wants to know. If the problem is a desire, a longing for adventure, the character roams the streets of the city in search of it, and because of his receptiveness is able to find it. Thus, the ultimate discovery of a solution invariably brings the character to a deeper understanding of himself, and although this understanding may not be directly stated, it is implied by the very nature of the conclusion.

All of these plot patterns—the cross, the triangular, the habit, and the quest—have in common the element of union, either where two paths intersect, as in the cross and triangular patterns, or where a path circles back to its starting point, as in the habit and quest patterns. At this point of union lies the surprise ending which is the hallmark of all Porter's stories. The key to the surprise, as has been shown, is the revelation of something hitherto unknown— an event that has already occurred or a truth of human nature that has lain hidden; frequently, but not always, this revelation takes the form of reversal.

In the cross patterns, the union occurs at an intersection of paths: in the cross-purposes and crossed paths patterns, the moment of revelation hinges on an action which has already occurred but is only now being revealed, and in the cross-identity pattern, it hinges on the stripping away of false identity and the exposition of characters' true natures. In the triangular pattern, the union also comes at an intersection, when path C crosses path A, completing the triangle. The union reveals a relationship which existed previously, unbeknownst to the reader, or (as in "The Social Triangle") one which occurs at that moment, giving previous relationships a profound significance. In the habit pattern, the union marks the closing of a circle, where the character returns to his own starting point, having strayed off on some temporary digression;

the revelation concerns the response to this change, and the meeting point reaffirms the security of routine. In the quest pattern, the union is also produced by a full circle, as the character ends up where he began; the revelation comes through the discovery of the solution within himself, a discovery which enlightens the character about his own nature.

Porter's stories are all designed with the ending as the central focus, as though, having devised an ending, Porter then wrote a story to accompany it, frequently scattering clues along the way that can reveal the ending to an observant reader. This tight craftsmanship, with all narrative events and elements leading directly to the planned conclusion, is the basis of Porter's style. The plot patterns delineated here help to illustrate just how Porter achieved his effect, although, as has been pointed out, much more is involved than just the story and the snappy twister.

Some critics, pointing to this mastery as also the source of his trickery, argue that such mechanical structure weakens Porter's stature as an artist. Such critical judgments are of course individual, but the purpose here is not so much to judge as to analyze. From the brief summaries cited in this chapter, weaknesses and contradictions are apparent in many of the stories. Still, it would be well to consider how Porter's skillfully executed plot patterns reflect the themes contained within them and how those themes are universal, expressed in the most ancient literature as well as the most modern. Bob Dylan has sung about "When I Paint My Masterpiece"; Bruce Springsteen voices the troubles, hopes, frustrations, and despairs of the working man; John Cheever and John Updike have both etched out the middle-aged, mundane routines of bored suburbanites. And fantasies such as spending a week's vacation among the wealthy are certainly not out of fashion.

The subjects Porter treats, then, are familiar, and the plot patterns themselves satisfy conventional expectations and draw upon conventional plot forms. In the first two stories of the cross-purposes pattern ("The Gift of the Magi" and "A Service of Love"), the problems facing the characters are solved through self-sacrifice, a quality which is emphasized by the author in his surprise ending. The third cross-purposes story ("The Love Philtre of Ikey Schoenstein"), based upon the traditional love triangle with its rivalry and jealousy, also concludes with the distinctive double surprise, and while the underdog Ikey loses the girl, the successful character wins her by honorable methods, so the outcome is satisfactory.

The crossed-paths pattern, another version of the traditional love story, with its separated lovers hopefully searching for each other, is also resolved satisfactorily, if not romantically, most of the time. While "The Furnished Room" does not end happily, it does end on a romantic note, since the frustrated young man dies for love, a death carried out in true Romeo and Juliet fashion, producing a noble though sad ending—followed by the typical Porter punch.

The cross-identity pattern achieves more profound effects through conventions than the other two cross patterns, touching upon the inner conflicts of human nature, presenting within one character two different identities. Countless pieces of literature have utilized this theme, from Shakespeare's plays to Mark Twain's tales of twins, whether in the form of moral conflict, psychological split, or spiritual struggle. Porter intensifies the effect by exposing this dual nature in two separate characters who then encounter one another by conventional means, such as sitting in the park or vacationing in a hotel.

In the patterns of the cross plot, then, Porter usually presents the complication at the opening of the story, with the pursuit of a solution serving as the plot development, ending with the ultimate resolution of the problem, a resolution which bears the unmistakable Porter touch. Occasionally, as with the cross-identity pattern, Porter withholds the complication until the end, merely presenting the situation and ensuing action so that it is the revelation of the complication which provides the twist and the purpose for the entire story.

In the triangular pattern, an episodic division is the common feature, but beyond that the plot structure may vary widely. All the stories are divided into segments, with the ending of the last segment holding the key which binds all the segments together, but where the complication is revealed, or whether one even exists, depends upon the story. In "Roses, Ruses and Romance," for example, segment one presents the situation, segment two develops the complication, and segment three resolves it. In "The Last Leaf," however, the complication comes first; it is further developed in segment two and satisfactorily resolved in segment three. In a story like "The Social Triangle," no real complication exists but just a series of interconnected incidents which are ironically unified with the last line of the story. All the stories, though, depend on that final, withheld piece of information for the completion of the picture.

The patterns of the habit plot draw strongly upon the traditional conflict between order and disorder, security and adventure, even though this conventional theme is embodied in rather mundane, amusing, even ridiculous incidents. Perhaps more than any other plot pattern, this one reflects Porter's style as a popular writer, for its theme and structure of recurrence embody the concept of formula underlying the author's stories and their appeal. The struggle between the "quest for order and the flight from ennui"[12] has shaped much literature, and has provided a basis of literary formulas, as Harry Berger points out:

Man has...a need for order, peace, and security,...for a familiar and predictable world, and for a life which is happily more of the same.... But...man positively needs anxiety and uncertainty, thrives on confusion and risk, wants trouble, tension, jeopardy, novelty, mystery....[13]

The tension this conflict arouses is the basis of the habit pattern, which reinforces the power of routine. In these plot patterns, the "predictable world" is usually stronger than the trouble or adventure that intercedes. The characters face a conflict, a desire to break from the routine, and yet when the opportunity arises they are unable to cope with that new freedom. As Cawelti points out, "If we seek order and security, the result is likely to be boredom and sameness. But rejecting order for the sake of change and novelty brings danger and uncertainty."[14]

The same conflict is evident in some stories of the quest pattern, for characters here seek adventure to shake off the cloud of boredom. The quest story follows a conventional, even archetypal pattern, as the character is confronted with a problem or question he seeks to solve, ventures forth in pursuit of the knowledge, and ultimately attains it—though upon his own shores. This quest is usually either a flight from ennui or a search born of curiosity, the character not being satisfied with the usual generality or explanation.

Thus the plot patterns Porter employs most frequently—the cross, the triangular, the habit, and the quest—incorporate the two essential elements of formulaic literature: convention and repetition. Conventionally, they are structured with settings and elements familiar to contemporary readers; they draw upon conventional situations, develop through a variety of methods, and conclude in a satisfying manner, with conventional values upheld and expectations fulfilled. Besides occurring repeatedly within the context of the urban stories, the plot patterns also imitate, with the use of cultural elements, plot patterns which are themselves conventional or archetypal. By employing conventional systems to illustrate cultural elements, and by creating his own pattern of repetition, Porter has established his urban short stories in the tradition of formulaic literature.

Chapter Four
Character Types

The recurrent use of stock characters in the same pattern of repetition and variation that his plots reflect constitutes the second major aspect of Porter's formulaic art. The characters who populate Porter's urban short stories share two common bonds aside from membership in the O. Henry repertoire: they are types rather than well-delineated individuals, and they are products, even embodiments, of the multi-faceted, impersonal city whose streets they inhabit and wander. Just as the plot structures can be classified into particular patterns upon which a number of variations are worked, so can the characters be identified as particular sorts of people and grouped accordingly, creating a gallery of faceless prototypes whose basic nature is defined by certain characteristics, differentiated only by a few quick strokes of invidivuality.

Unlike the plot patterns of these urban stories, which can even be translated into geometric designs, the characters elude distinct classification; they are, in fact, much more fluid because of shared characteristics. So any attempt to divide them must necessarily be arbitrary and not absolute, threatening, as Eugene Current-Garcia points out, to "break down under the pressure of overlapping."[1]

Porter's characters, in contrast to the living and breathing people of a writer like Henry James, are rather composites of class elements, structured types which the author calls upon repeatedly. The particular type or types he selects depend partly upon the plot pattern and the nature of the story, and they are usually described by representative traits rather than individual qualities. Thus, the reader meets Maisie, one of "3,000 girls in the Biggest Store" (1261), or Irving Carter, "painter, millionaire, traveller, poet, automobilist" (1262), the "bride who sat in the rocker with her feet resting upon the world" (1270), Ravenel "the traveler, artist and poet" (1312), or "Old Anthony Rockwall, retired manufacturer and proprietor of Rockwall's Eureka Soap" (53).

Frequently Porter himself classifies his characters as a means of description, defining them by membership in a species whose characteristics he enumerates to some degree. Thus, "Big Jim Dougherty was a sport" (1266), Nancy is "a shopgirl" (1366), and Vallance joins the "aristocracy of the public parks and even of the vagabonds" (1295). But since a character often exhibits the attributes of more than one class simultaneously, such categorizing as this is usually tenuous.

Just as the outcome of the plots can be anticipated due to their frequent and predictable repetition, so can the fates of certain Porter character types be reasonably surmised based upon the experiences of their predecessors, though the destinies of characters so protean in nature are less predictable than the more rigid plots. Still, some general assumptions can be made about particular types. The shopgirl, for example, meets one of two ends: either she is somehow "rescued" from her plight of poverty or she remains impoverished indefinitely through fate or her own foolishness; occasionally she might simply starve to death through no fault of her own—the cold harsh world is to blame. The domestic character type, whether husband or wife, will inevitably remain in the worn rut of his or her existence, despite some deviation which temporarily breaks the usual routine. This pattern too may be occasionally disrupted when the character type breaks the routine permanently by abandoning the domestic situation altogether. So the characters in Porter's stories follow certain patterns of existence, patterns which depend not upon the type of individuals they are, but rather upon the type of class they belong to ("class" here referring loosely to some kind of grouping, not necessarily social). These patterns of existence sometimes correspond to the patterns of the plots themselves, such as the domestic character, whose monotonous routine—which in itself defines him as a type—is embodied by the circular structure of the plot (the habit pattern).

But Porter's characters are not totally mechanical manipulations; they do possess some individuality, some particular characteristics—a brown mole, attractive eyes, a clever imagination—to distinguish them from other, similar types. Nevertheless, such distinction is subservient to assimilation, for Porter isn't really concerned with presenting and developing individual characters or with studying their thoughts and responses and exploring the changes they undergo; rather, he offers brief if shallow observations of them as representatives of human nature caught in different situations. It is the characteristics of a particular *type* of person which Porter deals with, not the qualities peculiar to a particular *person*. Porter writes not about the individual, but about the social creature:

Man in solitude made little appeal to O. Henry.... But man in society, his "humours" in the old sense, his whims and vagaries, his tragedies and comedies and tragi-comedies, his conflicts with individual and institutional forces, his complex motives, the good underlying the evil, the ideal lurking potent but unsuspected within—whatever entered as an essential factor into the social life of man and woman wrought a sort of spell upon O. Henry and found increasing expression in his art.[2]

As social creatures—specifically, as inhabitants of the city— Porter's characters share a second common bond. It is important to consider the city in defining these character types, for environment is a crucial element of their makeup and shaper of their destinies. The shopgirl, for example, is a figure of innocence subjected to the impersonal forces of industrialization; the tramp, usually a victim of circumstances, is a reflection of the city's downtrodden, lifetime resident of city parks, and regular member of the bread lines; the aristocrat, on the other hand, embodies the abundance and wealth found in the turn-of-the-century cities. Other Porter characters, such as the grafter, the Texan, the cowboy, and so forth, may reflect similar characteristics of human nature, but they too are clothed in a particular cultural garb. The traits displayed by Porter's urban characters—innocence, greed, generosity, or nobility, for example—are not peculiarly urban qualities; they may be found in characters of other locales as well, for indeed, they are universal character traits. But the means by which these traits are conveyed in the New York stories, the conditions under which they emerge, are directly related to the urban environment. Porter's characters, notes Harry Hansen, are "individual, part of the vast currents of the city's life,"[3] while Alphonso Smith claims that "the most thought-provoking aspect of O. Henry's portrayal of New York...lies in his attempt to isolate and vivify the character, the service, the function of the city. Streets, parks, squares, buildings, even the multitudinous life itself that flowed ceaselessly before him were to him but the outward and visible signs of a life, a spirit that informed all and energized all."[4]

Porter's characters can be typed by nationality (or pseudo-nationality): the Irishman, the Jew, the Bohemian; they can be typed by class: the lower, middle, and upper classes; or by vocation: the worker, the artist, the poet, the adventurer, the lover, and so forth. Acknowledging that classification is inevitably exclusive to some extent, a stratification that reflects both occupation and social position—and frequency of appearance, of course—should prove useful. Porter's characters can thus be grouped into six types: the shopgirl, the habitual character, the lover, the aristocrat, the plebeian, and the tramp. The fact that these categories obviously can intermingle is not so much a matter of an analysis breaking down under "the pressure of overlapping" as it is a matter of recognizing that Porter's character types are often ambiguous. Consequently, his shopgirls may also be lovers or plebeians, but in the stories where they appear, their primary identity is *as shopgirls*. The same is true of the other categories of characters.[5]

I

Of all the types that Porter created, his shopgirl is undoubtedly the most famous and the most revered, for "it is as the little shop-girl's true-knight-errant that O. Henry stands most vividly before us."[6] This is the character who appears most frequently in the urban stories, invariably arousing readers' sympathies, for even the most detached must feel compassion for her oppression.

The shopgirl exists—just barely—on her small income derived from waitress, department store or clerical work; she lives in a single-room flat with a gas burner and a few sticks of furniture, eating potatoes or, when prosperity smiles, a bit of side meat for dinner; she scrimps and saves for months on end to indulge herself in the pleasure of a new hat or dress. Usually she is alone, an orphan turned out into the "cold, cruel world" to make her way as best she can, but always she is independent, full of determination, and incessantly hopeful. Cinderella-like, she finds sustenance in dreams—of marrying a rich and handsome young man, or perhaps of winning fame and fortune on her own. Occasionally, she succumbs to the cold fate that pursues her, as does Eloise Vashner, who (though she is never seen) commits suicide in "The Furnished Room." But more often, frail though she may be, she withstands the buffeting winds of poverty and despair.

Porter condescendingly delineates this type in "The Trimmed Lamp," chiding the reader all the while for his or her expectations:

Nancy you would call a shop-girl—because you have the habit. There is no type; but a perverse generation is always seeking a type; so this is what the type should be. She has the high-ratted pompadour and the exaggerated straight front. Her skirt is shoddy, but has the correct flare. No furs protect her against the bitter spring air, but she wears her short broad cloth jacket as jauntily as though it were Persian lamb! On her face and in her eyes, remorseless type-seeker, is the typical shop-girl expression. It is a look of silent but contemptuous revolt against cheated womanhood; of sad prophecy of the vengeance to come. When she laughs her loudest the look is still there.... It is a look that should wither and abash man; but he has been known to smirk at it and offer flowers— with a string tied to them. (1366)

Although Porter has neatly side-stepped his own responsibility here, it is he who prompts the reader to be a "remorseless type-seeker," for, having created such expectations, he reinforces them again and again. Dulcie, in "An Unfinished Story," works in a department store, receiving six dollars a week; Maisie, of "A Lickpenny Lover," smiles "the shopgirl smile, and I enjoin you to shun it unless you are well fortified with callosity of the heart, caramels and a congeniality for the capers of Cupid" (1262); the half-starved waif discovered by Rudolf behind "The Green Door" tells a story that "was one of a thousand such as the city yawns at every day—the shopgirl's story of insufficient wages, further reduced by 'fines' that go to swell the store's profits" (66-67); The Girl From Sieber-Mason's on "The Ferry of Unfulfillment" wears her brown hair "neatly braided; her neat waist and unwrinkled black skirt were eloquent of the double virtues—taste and economy" (1471). Similar, sometimes identical, physical characteristics define all of Porter's shopgirls, so he is only chiding the reader for responding to a type which he himself has consciously perpetuated.

The shopgirl is marked by innocence; she is a poor player who must accept the hand Fate or Fortune deals her, exercising virtually no control in shaping her own destiny. In the grim and merciless grip of the city, she is apt to suffer many misfortunes, frequently physical ones such as starvation or malnutrition. Elsie, for example, in "The Skylight Room," becomes "too weak to light the lamp or to undress" (23). She falls upon her iron cot, "her fragile body scarcely hollowing the worn springs" (23); but ultimately she is rescued, at the brink of death, by her long-lost Prince Charming. The woefully pale, tottering vision of beauty that Rudolph Steiner discovers behind the green door accounts for her fainting spell by confessing that she has not eaten for three days, a victim of shameful wages, lost time due to illness, lost positions, lost hopes.

The misfortune that the shopgirl suffers might be spiritual rather than physical; she may be a victim of despair or loneliness, a condition which certainly would accompany hunger but not necessarily be attributed to it. Even if it is, the focus in this case is upon the mental despair, not the physical. Take, for example, Cecilia in "The Third Ingredient," pining away in the fear that the valiant and wealthy young man who a few days earlier had rescued her from an overboard suicide attempt will be unable to find her again, despite his vow that he would seek her out in the city. Or Florence in "Brickdust Row," who must meet men on the street because her tenement apartment house has no parlor entertainment; but, she says, "You get used to it" (1410). Even Elsie of "The Skylight Room," though a victim of physical hunger, is also spiritually starving for a lost lover named Billy Jackson, whom she addresses apostrophically every night in the form of a star; and when she finally collapses, she gazes at the star, murmuring, "You're millions of miles away.... But you kept where I could see you most of the time up there when there wasn't anything else but darkness to look at...." (23).

Although hunger and empty despair are ways of life for the shopgirl, they do not end her life, except on rare occasion. In most of Porter's urban stories, two disparate possibilities await the shopgirl: either she is rescued by some Prince Charming in *deus ex machina* style, or she faces a future which holds nothing but the dark promise of more loneliness and poverty.

The case of the convenient arrival is most evident in stories which are structured on the patterns of the cross plot, a structure which allows clues of the Prince Charming's existence to be planted—inscrutable though they may be—early in the story, keeping the arrival from being totally manipulated and thus artistically false. The cross pattern, remember, is focused through a number of sub-patterns on a final intersection or crossing of paths that harbors the surprise element, which in this case is of course the propitious arrival.

For example, take the earlier-discussed story "Springtime A La Carte," with the shopgirl type Sarah, who is not technically a shopgirl, since she freelances at home with her typewriter, but who possesses all the necessary attributes. Sarah is despondent— but not starving—because her betrothed lover from the country has not arrived with the first signs of spring as he had promised, and tears "from the depths of some divine despair rose in her heart and gathered to her eyes" (61). The sudden but not altogether unexpected arrival of the lover, which marks the critical element of crossing paths, transforms her tears into smiles, her despair into joy.

"The Skylight Room," mentioned earlier but not analyzed, offers another example of the shopgirl rescue couched in the cross pattern. Here Miss Elsie Leeson, "a very little girl, with eyes and hair that had kept growing after she had stopped" (20), comes to a boarding house in search of a cheap room. Like Sarah, she solicits typing jobs to pay her bills, an unreliable source of income, yet she is "gay hearted and full of tender, whimsical fancies" (21). Every night she gazes through her skylight at a steady blue star she calls Billy Jackson, and one night, having had no jobs and thus no meals, she collapses upon her cot; when she is discovered the next day, an ambulance is called, and the young doctor, upon learning her name, rushes up to the room and bears her down with the face "of one who bears his own dead" (24). The narrator closes the story with a reference to an item in the next morning's paper which reads, "Dr. William Jackson, the ambulance physician who attended the case, says the patient will recover" (24).

This story follows the pattern of the crossed paths, since an implied earlier union exists, followed by an unexplained divergence of paths, and finally the ultimate reunion, which also provides the timely rescue of the shopgirl from her plight. The arrival is sudden, unexpected, and suspiciously coincidental, although still some preparation has been made for it by passing mention of the missing lover.

The arrival of the rescuer is a bit more plausible in "The Third Ingredient," since the existence of the suitor is made clear from the start, along with the fact that he is consciously searching for Cecilia, who is despairing that he will ever find her. This story too follows the crossed-paths pattern, although it can almost be seen as a triangular pattern as well.

In the narrative, Cecilia, a slim, small artist with gold brown hair and plaintive eyes who rooms at the Vallambrosa Apartment House, is approached in the hall one evening by another resident, a shopgirl, Hetty Pepper, who is actually the initial character of the story. Hetty is preparing to cook her bit of rib beef into a stew when she encounters Cecilia washing two large potatoes at the hall sink. She invites her to throw them into the stew, and as they prepare supper in Hetty's room, with Hetty murmuring constant wishes for an onion to complete the feast, Cecilia breaks down into tears. Hetty, "who had accepted her rôle long ago" (692), offers the Shoulder To Cry On as the artist relates her story of how, a few days previous, she had jumped overboard from the ferry in a suicide attempt. A young man rescued her, tended to her, and tried to obtain her address, but she refused to supply it; he valiantly swore to find her anyway. Of course, he was wealthy as well. Hetty soothes the girl, and says to allow him more time, then goes out to obtain more water. Enroute again to the hall sink, she encounters a large onion clasped in the hand of a young man. In the process of persuading him to donate the onion to the cause, she discovers that he is the endeared young and rich suitor. And so Cecilia presumably faces a prosperous future, although the actual encounter between the two lovers is never shown.

Again, Cecilia is a starving young artist rather than a starving shopgirl, but she possesses the qualities which qualify her as a shopgirl type: small and frail, innocent and vulnerable, poverty-stricken. Like Sarah in "Springtime A La Carte" and Elsie in "A Skylight Room," she is a victim of misfortune: Sarah's is primarily spiritual, Elsie's is primarily physical, and Cecilia's is primarily spiritual, supplemented by physical. All three are succumbing to one or the other misfortune, making their vulnerability clear and pathetic. Thus it is relieving and satisfying for the reader when all three are rescued from this despair by the timely arrival of the knight in shining armor.

But the fairy tale ending of "The Third Ingredient" is marred, or at least made more grim, by a final bittersweet note. For although Cecilia apparently faces a happy-ever-after future, no such fate awaits Hetty, who is, rather ironically, the shopgirl in the story. But Hetty is not the vulnerable and pathetic figure of the usual shopgirl type. Physically she is different, "homely of countenance, with small contemptuous green eyes and chocolate colored hair, dressed in a suit of plain burlap and a common sense hat" (689). She is more hardened by experience and thus more capable of dealing with the world; thirty-three and motherly, just discharged from her job at the Biggest Store, she is a kind individual "who had not yet outlived the little pang that visited her whenever the head of youth and beauty leaned upon her for consolation" (693). She is a shoulder, a "sharp, sinewy shoulder; but all her life people had laid their heads upon it, metaphorically or actually, and had left there all or half their troubles" (692-93). And now, at the end of the story, she stands at the sink, peeling the onion and looking out at the gray roofs.

In this trio of stories, Porter has presented cultural embodiments of the archetypal damsel-in-distress theme, or innocence buffeted by the cold world. All three of these characters seem to be lost: Sarah and Cecilia are clearly separated from lovers they desperately seek; Elsie, whose struggle is a bit more valiant and pathetic, can be assumed, in the end, to have been separated from her lover too, judging by the latter's reaction when he discovers who the victim is. This confrontation between innocence and evil has long appealed to audiences, and in Porter's urban stories, the dilemma dons the garb of industrial America bound by threads of realism.

Touches of realism such as the portrait of Hetty in "The Third Ingredient" are especially sober, and serve to underscore the joyous fate of the Sarahs and Elsies and Cecilias. Porter dispenses these touches in small enough doses to remind the reader of a grim reality without spoiling the illusion of the other happy endings. Such a reminder also suggests "a firm basis of truth which the public sensed and approved,"[7] enlarging the appeal of Porter's stories.

The alternative fate of the shopgirl, even an innocent and vulnerable one, is similar to Hetty's: a continuing life of poverty and emptiness. The stories which lead up to this culmination are also built upon the cross pattern, although they do not strictly follow any one of the sub-patterns but rather employ elements of all three. The crossing of paths is intrinsic to these stories: the shopgirl meets a would-be rescuer, but no earlier acquaintance and subsequent separation are implied; these are chance encounters, like those in the cross-identity pattern. An element of misunderstanding, which is a kind of cross-purpose, prevents this encounter from leading to a happy ending for the two characters involved, although it is the shopgirl who appears to suffer the most. An element of lost opportunity is also involved, usually due to a verbal misunderstanding which results from a careful manipulation of dialogue on Porter's part. Such is the outcome, for example, in "The Ferry of Unfulfillment."

In this story, Claribel Colby, a shopgirl from Sieber-Mason's, is spotted in the homeward rush by the Man From Nome, who of course falls in love with her immediately, follows her on to the ferry—for she "belonged to that sad company of mariners known as Jersey commuters" (1471)—and secures a seat beside her. After convincing Claribel that he is not the stereotypical masher, he discourses to her about his wealth and his feelings toward her; she, meanwhile, exhausted from the day's work, falls asleep on his shoulder. Then, worried that she might want only his money, he asks her which she would prefer a man to have: love or money. She, deep in dreams of her counter work at Seiber-Mason's, replies, "Cash!" (1474) His abrupt departure wakens her, and she says, "Wonder what became of the White Wings?" (1474) Thus, her opportunity for marriage to a wealthy man and freedom from her drudgery vanishes with a chance remark, intensified by the pity of dramatic irony.

The same ending comes to Masie in "A Lickpenny Lover," who foolishly misinterprets a wealthy young customer's intentions. Masie is one of 3,000 girls in the Biggest Store, a lovely, lady-like blonde who proffers "the shopgirl smile" (1262). Irving Carter, "painter, millionaire, traveler, poet, automobilist," comes to buy a pair of gloves and falls in love for the first time in his life. He courts her for a few weeks, then proposes, offering her a life of one long holiday "where summer is eternal, where the waves are always rippling on the lovely beach and the people are happy and free as children" (1265), in far-away cities with palaces and towers, streets of water, temples and Japanese gardens and endless exotic sights. Poor Masie, however, rejects him, thinking he wants to take her to Coney Island. Thus it is her own foolishness and sad naivete which stave off happiness.

More somber and tragic is the outcome of a shopgirl like Florence in "Brickdust Row," a story which considers more seriously the plight of the shopgirl and the miserable conditions of her existence.

The story centers on Alexander Blinker, sole young heir of a deceased millionaire, who is bored and impatient with the business of legal paperwork. Detained from a vacation by the "confounded papers" (1405), he takes off on a jaunt to Coney Island, and on the ferry he meets an attractive young shopgirl named Florence, who has the usual frank gray eyes and pert little mouth. As they are returning after a day that is fascinating for Blinker and enchanting for Florence, a steamer crashes into the ferry and tears a hole in the side. The ferry threatens to sink, and as it inches toward the dock, Blinker expresses his feelings for Florence and learns about her style of meeting men. "Why don't you entertain your company in the house where you live?" he asks in jealous anger. "Is it necessary to pick up Tom, Dick and Harry on the streets?" (1409)

Her reply is pathetic:

"If you could see the place where I live you wouldn't ask that. I live in Brickdust Row. They call it that because there's red dust from the bricks crumbling over everything. I've lived there more than four years. There's no place to receive company. You can't have anybody come to your room. What else is there to do? . . . I meet a good many nice fellows at church. I go on rainy days—stand in the vestibule until one comes up with an umbrella. (1409-10)

The boat lands safely and they part, Blinker miserable and disgusted, cursing the church as he passes it. The next day he prepares to leave for his vacation, but the lawyer detains him by asking what he wants to do about certain tenements, in which his father had considered allowing the tenants to use one of the rooms for a parlor. It is Brickdust Row:

Blinker arose and jammed his hat down to his eyes.

"Do what you please with it," he said harshly. Remodel it, burn it, raze it to the ground. But, man, it's too late, I tell you. It's too late, it's too late, it's too late." (1410)

In all these stories, Porter employs the same character types as in the happy-ending stories. What changes is not the character but her fate. And if, as Smith suggests, Porter is concerned with human nature themes, it is only natural that he look at both sides of life, dealing with the negative as well as the positive aspects of human nature and of fate. In this way, the second group of stories balances out Porter's treatment of the shopgirl type. If the stories with happy endings respond to the reader's need to see innocence rescued and rewarded, then the stories with unhappy endings fulfill the yearning to see innocence elevated to nobility. One group promises the ultimate termination of human suffering, but the other acknowledges the ability of human nature to endure even when no such relief is in sight. One offers hope and promise for the future, but the other provides the assurance that, even without this glimmer of hope, the character will not succumb to evil forces. Shopgirls like Claribel and Florence, despite their unhappy prospects, will not settle for any two-bit masher; they possess too much pride and self-respect. Porter is thus drawing on the very basis of comedy and tragedy for his stories, presenting them in the context of contemporary class conditions. And because of this cultural approach—which certainly accounts for much of his popular appeal—Porter hovers on the outskirts of social commentary, although he never really commits himself. He does not make a serious attempt at reform in his literature, but he does come close enough to merit notice.

A story like "Brickdust Row" reflects the grim living conditions of the shopgirl and the careless abandon of her wealthy landlord who prospers at her expense. Blinker is depicted as a bored, resentful landlord who feels needlessly bothered by the business of property. Indeed, he does not even know what he owns, nor does he really care:

The Blinker wealth was in lands, tenements, and hereditaments, as the legal phrase goes. Lawyer Oldport had once taken Alexander in his little pulmonary gasoline runabout to see the many buildings and rows of buildings that he owned in the city. For Alexander was sole heir. They had amused Blinker very much. The houses looked so incapable of producing the big sums of money that Lawyer Oldport kept piling up in the banks for him to spend. (1405)

He is not aware that he owns Brickdust Row, although for five years his lawyer has been nagging him about it, trying to suggest the reforms. Although Blinker has now learned firsthand of the conditions its residents suffer, and although his millions could assuage these conditions, he harshly and disgustedly turns his back on the whole affair and escapes to the North Woods.

Porter delineates these conditions in several stories, more drastically in some than in others, but his purpose seems more to be a consistent portrayal of the shopgirl type and her life than any serious efforts at condemnation and reform. This is not to say that Porter harbored no conscious intentions of exposing this reality or sincere hopes for seeing it changed. His awareness of the real-life shopgirls's true plight is evident, and indeed, he drew upon this knowledge for his stories. But he simply presents the conditions and goes no further, implying criticism but stopping short of actual reproval. His stories offer narrative description, focusing on the "typical" abode of the shopgirl, with the unfavorable presentation usually serving more to arouse the reader's sympathy than his ire, intended more to complete a picture than to condemn a social condition.

Elsie Leeson, in "A Skylight Room," is escorted to the fourth floor and the skylight room, which "occupied 7 x 8 feet of floor space in the middle of the hall. On each side of it was a dark lumber closet." Inside was "an iron cot, a washstand and a chair. A shelf was the dresser. Its four bare walls seemed to close in upon you like the sides of a coffin. Your hand crept to your throat, you gasped, you looked up as from a well—and breathed once more" (19-20). Such a description, grimly realistic though it may be, is fine artistic preparation for Elsie's suffocating encounter with death later in the story.

Description also arouses sympathy for Dulcie, the unfortunate little heroine of "An Unfinished Story," who lives on six dollars a week: two dollars and sixty cents for the week's meals, sixteen cents for the papers, two dollars for the rent, not counting the need for clothes and occasional pleasures. She lives, of course, in a furnished room: "There is this difference between a furnished room and a boarding house. In a furnished room, other people do not know it when you go hungry" (73). It contains the usual couch-bed, dresser, table, washstand, and chair.

The same is true for Maisie in "A Lickpenny Lover," courted by wealthy Irving Carter. But Carter does not know the shopgirl:

He did not know that her home is often either a scarcely habitable tiny room or a domicile filled to overflowing with 'kith and kin. The street corner is her parlor, the park is her drawing room; the avenue is her garden walk; yet for the most part she is as inviolate mistress of herself in them as is my lady inside her tapestried chamber. (1264)

The squalor of her living conditions is thus another facet contributing to the composite picture of the shopgirl. All these elements taken together—physical appearance and moral fortitude, working situation, and living conditions—define the shopgirl as a character type, with occasional distinguishing characteristics thrown in to individualize her. The shopgirl type reappears over and over in Porter's urban stories, a fact which in itself invalidates the author's criticism of the reader as a "remorseless type seeker." On the contrary, this repeated performance allows the reader to recognize her as a familiar type and to arrive at certain expectations about her fate. Further, using such a character type reinforces Porter's repeated use of identical plot patterns, providing a unity in treatment of plot and characters, and thus an artistic unity in these stories.

For the reader, the shopgirl symbolizes innocence and endurance; she is a focus for pathos, and in her ultimate outcome, can satisfy the reader's need for comedy or for tragedy. If she is rescued and lives "happily ever after," then the reader can draw satisfaction from that conventional theme of innocence and misery requited. If she is not rescued, and can only face bravely toward the future, then the reader has been reassured that, despite adversity, even frail human nature will endure and survive. And if, as happens only rarely, the shopgirl succumbs to fate (as Eloise Vashner in "The Furnished Room," who commits suicide), the reader has the satisfaction of knowing that she died nobly and is now free from all suffering, and the reader can also feel assured that her action was justified by her misery.

II

Porter's compulsion to write about habit, reflected in the plot pattern examined earlier, is further reflected in the character types which can be found in those plots, types which, because of their lifestyle and routine, can be labelled the habitual character. The habitual character usually lives in a flat—which is as typical as the characters who occupy it—and follows a daily routine that reeks of domesticity and unmitigated boredom. The character types who fall into the category of habit are usually husbands and wives molded by years—sometimes only months—of uneventful marriage brimming with ennui. In a story involving these character types, one of the partners, usually the husband but occasionally the wife, yearns for some deviation from the dull routine, but when his wish comes true, the change only serves to reinforce the power of his previously despised cycle. So locked are these characters into the groove and routine of marriage that it is amusing to watch them veer from it temporarily.

The main character from "The Complete Life of John Hopkins" is representative of the habitual character:

John Hopkins was like a thousand others. He worked at $20 per week in a 9-story, red brick building at either Insurance, Buckle's Hoisting in Five Lessons, or Artificial Limbs. It is not for us to wring Mr. Hopkins's avocation from these outward signs that be. (1257)

Mrs. Hopkins, too, is "like a thousand others," though described in much more detail:

The auriferous tooth, the sedentary disposition, the Sunday afternoon wanderlust, the draught upon the delicatessen store for home-made comforts, the furor for department store marked-down sales, the feeling of superiority to the lady in the third floor front who wore genuine ostrich tips and had two names over her bell, the mucilaginous hours during which she remained glued to the window sill, the vigilant avoidance of the installment [sic] man, the tireless patronage of the acoustics of the dumbwaiter shaft—all the attributes of the Gotham flat-dweller were hers. (1257-58)

So routine are their lives that John Hopkins barely bats an eyelash when, as he is purchasing a cigar at the corner stand, he is whisked momentarily into a bygone world of romance and chivalry.

The same kind of routine binds the habitual characters of "The Pendulum." John Perkins drifts slowly home from the subway after work—slowly because there "are no surprises awaiting a man who has been married two years and lives in a flat. As he walked, John Perkins prophesied to himself with gloomy and downtrodden cynicism the foregone conclusions of the monotonous day" (1383). He knows that his typical domestic wife will "meet him at the door with a kiss flavored with cold cream and butter scotch" (1383). Perkins, like the typical, simple-minded husband flat-dweller, is "not accustomed to analyzing his emotions" (1386), but when he arrives home to find Katy gone and the expected routine convoluted, he is confused: his wish has come true; the "hymenal strings that had curbed him always when the Frogmore flats had palled upon him were loosened" (1386). When Katy returns unexpectedly, the wheels turn, everything falls back into place, and he slips back with relief into the appropriate cog.

So too with Mr. and Mrs. McCaskey, who pause from their domestic battle of crockery and dinner plates to cluck sympathetically over the disappearance of Mrs. Murphy's little boy, drawing affectionately towards one another and then, when the crisis has passed picking back up where they left off. Or Mr. and Mrs. Fink in "A Harlem Tragedy," he a sedentary husband, "permeated with the curse of domesticity" (1439), she longing for him to beat her up, tired of all the "tame rounds with her sparring partner" (1439). But so ensconced is Mr. Fink in his mild, plodding life that when she attempts to provoke him into brutal action, he, instead of responding with recreant fists, washes the clothes for her.

An odd, darkly satirical variation of the habitual character type is presented in "A Comedy in Rubber," in the persons of William Pry and Violet Seymour of the "rubber tribe," those "devotees of curiosity" who swarm like flies "about the scene of an unusual occurrence" (1282). William and Violet (whose surnames are good examples of Porter's razor-edged wit) meet in the street where a man has been run over by a brewery wagon, and it is love at first sight. After enjoying a short romance of rubbering together, gazing hand-in-hand at malformed boot-blacks and fallen window cleaners, they set a June wedding. When the day of the wedding arrives, however, the designated hour comes and goes but no Violet or

William shows. Finally, two crushed creatures are discovered beneath the feet of the mob of onlookers: "William Pry and Violet Seymour, creatures of habit, had joined in the seething game of the spectator, unable to resist the overwhelming desire to gaze upon themselves entering, as bride and bridegroom, the rose-decked church" (1285).

All these characters are slaves of habit, so conditioned by their various routines that they cannot break them if they try. Although some, such as John Perkins, resent being prisoners of habit and yearn to break free, they cannot renounce the ties even when the opportunity arises. But a character such as the husband in "Memoirs of a Yellow Dog" does cast off the shackles of habit, although until the very moment that he does, he had never given any thought to such an action. In this sense he deviates from the normal action of the habitual character.

The story is narrated from the point of view of a dog who lives in an ordinary flat with the ordinary husband and wife characters. She, the wife of habit, spends her day with

Laura Jean Libbey, peanut brittle, a little almond cream on the neck muscles, dishes unwashed, half an hour's talk with the iceman, reading a package of old letters, a couple of pickles and two bottles of malt extract, one hour peeking through a hole in the window shade into the flat across the air-shaft—that's about all there is to it. (47)

He, the henpecked husband, is "a little man with sandy hair and whiskers" who "wiped the dishes and listened to my mistress tell about the cheap, ragged things the lady with the squirrel skin coat on the second floor hung out on her line to dry" (47).

When Husband takes the dog out for his usual night walk, the dog leads him into a saloon, much to Husband's surprise, where, after a few hot Scotches, he begins to ruminate and decides that he's had enough of the habit-scarred domestic life. He says to his dog, "If I ever see that flat anymore, I'm a flat, and if you do you're flatter; and that's no flattery. I'm offering 60 to 1 that Westward Ho wins out by the length of a dachshund" (49).

The habitual character type fulfills two major functions. The first bears a direct relationship to the plot structure in which he is generally found. The character's pattern of repetition, deviation, and return to the usual repetition corresponds directly to the circular pattern of the plot, in which the action ends at the same place it began, having undergone some kind of digression from the routine. If the plot pattern is visualized as a circle (see Figure 6, chapter 3), then the character is traveling around that circle towards the culmination of the story. Thus, Porter has fused his character type with his plot pattern to create a unified effect in these stories.

The second function of the habitual character type lies in his relationship to the reader. This character symbolizes security and stability, the assurance that, despite change and upheaval, order will prevail in the end. But he also embodies the yearning spirit who longs to break free from his "bonds," only to discover that they weren't bonds at all. Like the persona of a popular song, when he achieves freedom, he finds himself "looking back and longing for the freedom of my chains."[8] Thrust into a sudden adventure or unexpected situation, the habitual character takes the reader through a vicarious experience which promises the certainty of ultimate return to the normal. Since the desire for order and for the security of repetition is a basic human need, sudden changes and deviations from routine can be disturbing and unsettling, but when experienced within the secure, predictable limits of a short story (or other artistic form), they can be enjoyed without fear or uncertainty.

This tension between order and chaos, between security and adventure, is inherent to human nature—as well as to human existence and to the natural world. Porter has clothed an archetypal conflict in cultural dress, presenting the universal human struggle in terms of the domestic situation. This fundamental conflict is what provides Porter's characters with zest, for Porter

sees two men in conflict in every one of us, the man who would spiritually succeed and the man who would materially succeed; and though he has little hope of the former winning, and indeed finds all the cards packed against his success, he knows that the strange little puppet, who is himself you and I, will keep on fighting against the odds eternally.[9]

Thus, the character type marked by habit, who experiences the common struggle between a need for security and a desire for adventure, and who faces the universal uncertainty of coping with change, enables the reader to vicariously experience the cycle of order—desire—conflict—restoration to order without having to endure the worries that invariably accompany it. The habitual character's frequent appearance in Porter's stories and his predictable performance—despite an occasional deviation in action and outcome—marks him as another type upon which Porter recurrently draws, and one with which readers can quickly become familiar.

III

A third character type, more encompassing and less clearly definable than these first two, is the lover, which includes both the married and unmarried. The most distinguishing feature of this character type is an overwhelming love for one's partner, whether wife or girlfriend, husband or boyfriend, and the overriding concern that he or she be happy. The lover is defined not simply by his or her status as a husband or boyfriend, wife or girlfriend, but rather by the attitude toward and treatment of the other partner. Thus, for example, although the characters of "The Pendulum" and "The Complete Life of John Hopkins" are husband and wife in both cases, it is not their relationship that is important so much as the routine that they have become ensconced in; the emphasis there is on habit rather than love.

Unlike the shopgirl type, the lover is not defined by physical characteristics. The character might be male or female, married or single, and fit a number of widely different descriptions. Ikey Schoenstein, for example, a timid, weak-kneed morsel in the presence of a woman, is a far cry from Kid McGarry, the undauntable prize fighter of "Little Speck of Garnered Fruit." Yet both are consumed by a passionate love for some woman. Ikey concocts a sleeping potion to thwart the plans of his rival and keep Rosie for himself; Kid McGarry, when his new bride absently says, "I think I would like a peach" (1270), is off without a word, for "the crook of her little finger could sway him more than the fist of any 142-pounder in the world" (1270). And though he has to search all over town and ultimately bust a gambling operation to secure the prize, he does not return home without the peach. "So rode the knights back to Camelot after perils and high deeds done for their ladies fair. The kid's lady had commanded him and he had obeyed" (1273).

Sometimes, however, the lover characters of different stories are quite similar. The most obvious examples here are the two married couples of "The Gift of the Magi" and "A Service of Love," two stories built upon the cross-purposes plot pattern, so that their actions, too, correspond almost exactly. Both are young, recently married couples deeply in love; both live in flats on meagre incomes; both are so totally content with one another that life is pleasant even in a dim, dripping flat, and their mutual love leads them to make great sacrifices for the happiness of the other. The couple in "The Gift" are named Della and Jim; the couple in "A Service" are named Delia and Joe. Both perform some action without the other partner being aware of it, and both turn out in the end to be working for the benefit of the other partner.

Porter works an amusing twist on the newlywed couple by employing the "forgetful husband" type. In stories like "From the Cabby's Seat" and "Romance of a Busy Broker," the information that the couple are married is withheld until the end. The first story concerns a cabby who, drunk in the revelry of his own wedding feast, picks up a fare, drives her around all night, and then, discovering that she has no money to pay him, trots her down to the police station. There he abashedly discovers that it is his new bride he has been driving, awkwardly introducing her to the captain to cover his mistake.

In the second tale, a harried broker denies that he ever asked for a new stenographer to replace the one he's had for a year, and brusquely sends away an Agency candidate. Caught in the fierce rush of business, he plows through his work; then, during a lunchtime lull, works up the courage to ask his stenographer to marry him. She replies, "Don't you remember Harvey? We were married last evening at 8 o'clock in the Little Church around the Corner" (88).

Here the emphasis lies neither on the marital bliss nor on routine, but on the humorous absent-mindedness of the husband. Offering an inventive twist on the newlywed theme, the stories at the same time reveal yet another aspect of human nature so easily recognized.

The lovers who are not married display the same strong desire to be with one another as those who, like Della and Jim, are married. Frequently they are separated for some unavoidable reason, and their efforts are geared towards establishing a reunion, an effort which often produces the pattern of the crossed-paths plot. This is the case, for example, with the young Irish pair in "Tobin's Palm," or the wistful typist and the ruddy farmer of "Springtime A La Carte." In each story, one partner is searching for the other, and each ends happily as the reunion finally occurs, though the emphasis differs in each story. In "Tobin's Palm," the focus is on Tobin searching for Katy, whose existence is known but who is never actually shown. In "Springtime," on the other hand, the emphasis is on Sarah, who is waiting to be found by Walter, whose existence is also made known, but who appears only at the end of the story.

Although these cases of separation result in happy endings, such is not always the case with the lovers. The separation may ultimately culminate in tragedy, such as the Romeo and Juliet love-despair of "The Furnished Room." A different sort of tragedy ends the idyllic love affair in "The Memento," where a young actress, having renounced stage life and an act which exposed her to the pawing, lecherous hands of men, moves to a small Long Island village and becomes engaged to a young minister, only to learn that the subject of an ideal love he had once felt for a woman "far above" him, was herself (1362). The memento he keeps of her is the garter which the girl used to kick off during her act, and when she discovers this, she packs up and returns to the city.

The unmarried lover might also be frustrated in his attempt to secure the affections of another, as Robert Gillian in "One Thousand Dollars," who cheerfully sacrifices all his money to secure the happiness of his uncle's young ward, knowing that she is not equally enamored of him; or the chemist of "The Love Philtre of Ikey Schoenstein," who, despite his efforts to thwart the young woman's marital plans, loses her to his rival; or the poet Ravenel in "Roses, Ruses and Romance," who briefly clasps the true fulfillment of romantic love only to have it dissolved by the cold reality of modernism.

Again, the motivation of these character types serves to enforce the development of the plots. The actions of Della and Jim, Delia and Joe, impelled by love for the other, create the cross-purposes pattern of the plot. The attempts of characters like Tobin and Walter to locate their lost lovers lead to the crossed-paths pattern. In a story like "Roses, Ruses and Romance," the amorous desires of the poet Ravenal expose the existence of a triangular pattern— in this case, the proverbial love triangle. So the character type of the lover is apparently not limited to any particular plot pattern; in fact, the type appears so frequently in Porter's urban stories that it can be found in virtually any pattern, except the habit type. By its very nature, the habit pattern is focused upon something more mundane than the mutual feelings of two lovers, even though their relationship is, to some extent, important.

All of these characters symbolize love—its perseverance, its generosity, its undauntedness. They personify the concept of self-sacrifice and the theme that "love conquers all," satisfying the reader's need to see selflessness (which is also a kind of innocence) rewarded and to see the lover's search fulfilled. In the process of satisfying this need, the stories weave a mild suspense, raising soap-opera sorts of tensions for the reader: "Will Jim still love Della without her beautiful hair?" Or "Will Walter come and rescue Sarah from her miserable menu-filled life?" Or "Will Tobin find Katy as the fortune-teller seemed to imply?" When these uncertainties are happily resolved, the reader can breathe a sigh of contented relief, secure in the assurance that the power of love still reigns.

But as with the shopgirl character type, the audience's need for tragedy is also met, with the stories that do not end happily. In a story like "The Furnished Room," love is still dominant, as the young man commits suicide after failing to find the woman he loves. This story reflects the same expression of love as *Romeo and Juliet* and the same nobility of character, except that whether Eloise died for the same love is uncertain. A story such as "The Memento" asserts the dominance of self-respect, and despite its unhappy ending, it satisfies the conventional expectation that principles be placed above even personal happiness. A story like "The Love Philtre of Ikey Schoenstein," though designed to gear the reader's sympathies toward Ikey, is too amusing to be tragic, and while the reader might feel that Ikey should win Rosie because of his pure intentions, he can, by the end of the story, feel that Chunk's triumph is justified, since he abandons his underhanded scheme in favor of an honorable one.

Thus, the character type of the lover responds to the reader's desire to see love, honor, and virtue prevail. Through sacrifice and perseverance, the character arouses the reader's sympathy and earns his own just reward. Through dignity and sincerity, he asserts the nobility and value of principle. Virtue and sentiment are focused in this character type and are developed in the plot structure in which he appears, resulting in a fusion that produces a tale of sentiment and sacrifice, a "love story," a narrative form which has long held appeal for readers of all ages.

IV

The aristocrat and the plebeian represent the New York class extremes. Here are the prince and the pauper of O. Henry's Bagdad, the rich and the poor man of his stories. As members of society, these two types are widely separated by an unbridgeable financial chasm, but as members of the human race they are in many respects alike.

The aristocrat is marked by his wealth. Usually a young character, sometimes middle-aged, and infrequently elderly, the aristocrat has more money than he knows what to do with, a fortune which is inherited, not earned through some sudden windfall. Consequently, in contrast to the poverty-stricken characters of the lower classes, he can afford to be nonchalant towards money, as Gillian in "One Thousand Dollars," who finds that sum bothersome, or Blinker in "Brickdust Row," who does not even know, or care about, the sources of his wealth. The aristocrat travels in chauffer-driven cars, eats at fine restaurants, and frequents country clubs, art galleries, theatres, and other upper-class habitats. Born into society, he has "everything a man could want—power, grace, and style,"[10] yet he displays a jaded, overriding disregard for money and the lifestyle it engenders. In the code of values by which he guides his life, money comes last, yielding to the more important values of love, honor, and dignity. This attitude is distinctive to the aristocrat, and surfaces repeatedly in Porter's character creations.

Despite a life of comfort and glamour, the aristocrat is sated with the incessant round of clubs and dinners and social events, and by the pretentiousness which pervades such activities. In the story "From Each According to His Ability," Vuyning leaves his club, wearied by the ennui of routine, and is delighted when a shady crook approaches him on the street: "He was hungry for something out of the ordinary, and to be accosted by this smooth-faced, keen-eyed low-voiced athletic member of the under world, [sic] with his grim yet pleasant smile, had all the taste of an adventure to the convention-weary Vuyning" (1353). Or John Reginald Forster of "The Venturers," who is a "Venturer by nature, but convention, birth, tradition, and the narrowing influences of the tribe of Manhattan had denied him full privilege" (1615). Sometimes, in order to further escape the bonds of class limitation, the aristocrat disguises himself as a common clerk or shopgirl, just as the lower class characters disguise themselves as wealthy, high society members in order to enjoy the enviable pleasures of that lifestyle for a short time. This mutual disguise, usually occurring simultaneously, provides the basis for the cross-identity plot pattern discussed earlier.

The young man in "While the Auto Waits," for example, passes himself off as a restaurant employee while conversing with a peasant girl who is parading as a woman of society. In this story, however, the disguise does not lead anywhere, having no apparent effect on the young man. At the end of the story, he simply picks her book up from the ground, then tosses it aside, steps into the limousine, and directs his chauffer to the club.

More consequential is the momentary masquerade of Miss Marion in "Lost on Dress Parade." She wears the costume of a shopgirl to her dressmaker's boutique in order to have it worked on, but while returning home, she twists her ankle and is approached helpfully by a young man of respectable appearance. Accepting his assistance, she does not disclose her true position but implies by silence—to him and to the reader—that she is only a working girl. The young man, however, Towers Chandler, *is* a working man, treating himself to his periodic "night on the town": every ten weeks he purchases a "gentleman's evening" (91), dressing as a millionaire and dining in luxury. He prates to Miss Marion of "clubs, of teas, of golf and riding and kennels and cotillions and tours abroad," but when she asks if he has any work that interests him, he replies, "We do-nothings are the hardest workers in the land" (94). At the end of the story, when she returns to her handsome mansion, Marion tells her sister she could love a man who fits Chandler's description exactly, if "he had an ambition, an object, some work to do in the world." But "the man who lives an idle life between society and his clubs—I could not love a man like that," she confides (96).

Unknowingly, she has encountered the very kind of man she *could* love, and had she not disguised her identity, she would have discovered that. So too would Chalmers, had he not disguised his as well. In the end, she ironically expresses displeasure with the lifestyle of her own class, a displeasure which presumably induces her to don the shopgirl's garb in the first place.

This disregard for money is common to all of Porter's aristocrat character types. Love usually takes precedence as a value on their scales, for without it, despite the millions they possess, they are unhappy. Such is the case with young Gillian in "One Thousand Dollars," who cheerfully and cleverly arranges for his thousands to go to the young orphan lady he loves, even though he is well aware that she has rejected him. Or Blinker in "Brickdust Row," who, under the influence of love's elixir, "no longer saw a mass of vulgarians seeking gross joys" in the mobs at Coney Island, but rather looked "clearly upon a hundred thousand true idealists" (1407). He loses this love in the end, but appropriately that loss is due to his wealth.

A humorously ironic twist to this "money can't buy love" philosophy is presented in "Mammon and the Archer." Richard Rockwall, son of a soap manufacturer, is in love with a young woman of equal stature who is "part of the stream" (55) that turns the social mill, and whose every minute is accounted for. He cannot hope to get enough time alone with her to propose before she sails to Europe the next day for a two-year stay. He is allowed only to meet her that night and drive her to the theatre, a six-or eight-minute journey at the most. Young Rockwall glumly touts the uselessness of money in this situation. His cunning father, however, a firm believer in aristocratic possibilities, pays off a driver to arrange a traffic jam which delays the cab for two hours, buying Richard time enough to be successful in his amours. Rockwall is the epitome "of O. Henry's type of the self-made American business tycoon: he knows that money talks, even in the affairs of the heart."[11]

Carson Chalmers, aristocrat of "A Madison Square Arabian Night," seeks love in a somewhat different manner. Having received a photograph of his wife in the mail, accompanied by a letter filled with "poisoned barbs" (1374) and innuendoes about her from another woman, he is plagued by doubts. (That the picture is of his wife and that she is traveling in Europe is not revealed until the end of the story.) He has his butler select at random a homeless man from the bed line outside, because he "felt the inefficacy of conventional antidotes to melancholy," needing something "high-flavored and Arabian" (1375).

The man consequently ushered in turns out to be Sherrard Plumer, a once-successful artist who has failed because he revealed more honesty in portraits than people could bear. Chalmers has Plumer make a sketch from the photograph he received; then, afraid to look at it, he calls in an artist from the upstairs apartment, who claims it shows the face of an angel, restoring Chalmers' faith and happiness. Apparently, then, Chalmers values the love and fidelity of his wife far more than his wealth, and without that emotional stability, it is clear that his money would be worthless.

This judgment of values is put to the ultimate test when the aristocrat must choose between love and money, and the outcome is always the same. Not one of Porter's urban aristocrats ever rejects love in order to retain his status of wealth. The richness of love is too important to him, as is the dignity of honor and self-respect, and the freedom to run his own life as he chooses. If, having been disinherited for loving an "unacceptable" woman, the aristocrat is ultimately restored to favor, it is not because he has relented in the matter and agreed to give up the woman; rather, it is because the disapproving relative—father, uncle, etc.—has relinquished his position and agreed to comply with the young man's decision.

Such is the case with Vallance, who finds himself in Madison Square Park because he has not a cent for food or bed or streetcar fare, and all "because an uncle had disinherited him for seeing a certain girl" (1295). He becomes acquainted with another bum who, coincidentally, is his disinherited cousin (unrecognized), who was to be re-inherited in the place of Vallance. By the end of the story, however, the cousin-bum is again disinherited, and Vallance is restored to order.

Kerner in "The Fool-Killer" finds himself in a similar situation, although it is he who cuts himself off from his wealthy father and keeps the girl. Kerner is an artist who pursues his life in a studio, existing as best he can on his art, and again, by the end of the story, through the help of his friend who is operating under the

influence and illusion of old folklore legends, Kerner is restored
to his father's goodwill and good fortune.

But Murray in "According to Their Lights" rejects the offer
to be reinstated as inheritor when it hinges on his acceptance of
his uncle's values. When the uncle's messenger locates Murray and
informs him of the forgiveness, Murray asks, " 'And the little
matrimonial arrangement?' " The uncomfortable messenger replies:

"Why—er—well, of course, your uncle understand—expects that the engagement
between you and Miss Vanderhurst shall be—"
"Good night," said Murray, moving away.
"You madman!" cried the other, catching his his arm. "Would you give
up two million on account of—"
"Did you ever see her nose, old man?" asked Murray, solemnly.
"But listen to reason, Jerry. Miss Vanderhurst is an heiress, and—"
"Did you ever see it?"
"Yes, I admit that her nose isn't—"
"Good night!" said Murray. "My friend is waiting for me. I am quoting
him when I authorize you to report that there is 'nothing doing.' Good night."
(1450)

Most of these stories are built on the cross-identity pattern or
some variation of it. The role of the character has been reversed
from aristocrat to beggar, and is ultimately either reversed back
to its initial position or is offered to be so reversed but rejected.
In the context of such a pattern, the emphasis in the stories is
placed upon the responses and reactions of the aristocrat character
to his ultimate fate, whether it is restoration or final rejection. And
it is this decision which is most significant in the stories. The
aristocrat is a kind of hero, for he reasserts the nobility of human
nature by not succumbing to temptation. He embodies the struggle
between material comfort and moral righteousness, the conflict
between upholding one's principles or casting them aside in favor
of simple conformity. He becomes a hero by choosing the path
he believes in rather than the one that is easiest, identifying himself
as a character of honor rather than of greed. The aristocrat satisfies
the reader's wish to see temptation conquered and principle upheld,
even in the face of wretched living conditions and an uncertain
future.

Among the urban aristocrats of Porter's stories, then, wealth and class—both inherited—are the distinguishing factors, and an ironic dissatisfaction with their lives marks their natures. Beyond these fundamental characteristics, a number of variations might be found. The aristocrat may be an adventure seeker from the unfulfilling, dull life of the rich; he may lack fulfillment because of the vital but missing ingredient of love; he may be disinherited and end up as a tramp on the street. All of these elements place him with other Porter characters in the arena of the human race. Wealth and status, both artificial endowments, set him apart, but never does Porter present a class snob who refuses to associate with the plebeians that are the source of his wealth. Rather, he has his characters don the garb of lower-class men and move about among them; he has them fall in love with characters of lower stature; he has them willingly step down from their aristocratic thrones for the sake of some overriding principle. Thus, the focus of Porter's portrayal is not so much on the characters as wealthy members of the upper class, but as wealthy members who are not possessed by their wealth, who are at any time willing to sacrifice that wealth for a moral value. That they are willing to abdicate from this luxurious lifestyle without qualm makes them admirable. For Porter they represent a class nobility, but more importantly, they represent human nobility.

V

The plebeian, or the lower-class New Yorker, is the antithesis of the aristocrat. Here is the man on the streets of Richard Cory's town who works in his factories and lives in his rooming houses. Like the aristocrat, the plebeian is set apart by his social and economic status; he dwells in poverty, surrounded by other uncultured workers and immigrants of the melting pot. The plebians are the shopgirls, who barely maintain sustenance or who survive a bit more comfortably on a meagre salary; they are the Ikey Schoensteins who derive their pleasures from wishing on stars; they are the clerks who—wishing they could be Richard Cory—trade two months' salary for a night as a gentleman or a lady, and the struggling young couples whose love for one another nourishes and sustains them. They are the husbands, wives, and lovers, the workers and the tramps who constitute the masses to which Porter seems so drawn.

For the most part, they make the best of their lives, some even preferring the simplicity of the tenement life to the pretentiousness and snobbery of higher class life (as does Katy in "A Philistine in Bohemia," who tells her suitor, "Sure, I'll marry wid ye. But why didn't ye tell me ye was the cook? I was near turnin' ye down for bein' one of them foreign counts!" (1352), others accepting only with grim bitterness their stations in life, cursing the life they're living.

The plebeian character type also encompasses street gangs whose actions and diversions often reflect their cultural condition and whose members are held in perpetual suspicion by the police because of their "serious occupation" of separating "citizens from their coin and valuables" (1415). When "Kid" Brady, the vainest, strongest, wariest, most successful plotter in the "Stovepipe" gang in "Vanity and Some Sables," having sworn to amend his ways, presents his girl Molly with a set of Russian sables, and concurrently a wealthy woman's expensive sables disappear from a house where the Kid had fixed the water pipes, he is immediately suspected. It turns out, however, that the sables the Kid bought cost only $21.50, a fact his pride would not let him reveal.

Porter's treatment of the plebeian, as with most of his other characters, is sentimental, suggesting a sympathetic approach to what was in reality a genuine threat of urban crime and violence. He romanticizes the gang members and their relationship to other members of society. Emerson in "From Each According to His Ability" is one of a "number of silent, pale-faced men who are accustomed to stand, immovably, for hours, busy with the file blades of their penknives, with their hat brims on a level with their eyelids" (1353), but to the naive and bored Vuyning he holds the promise of adventure. The inherent danger of the criminal is further ridiculed as Vuyning soberly advises him on the intricacies of proper haberdashery, and is finally negated altogether as the criminal, now aligned on the right track, heads west for a new, reformed life.

The portrayal is equally sympathetic in "Past One At Rooney's," a tale of romance blooming amidst the rubble and degradation of street life. Cork McManus, who a week earlier had knifed a rival gang member, and Fanny—alias Ruby—who regularly slips bribes to the policeman on the beat to look the other way, meet at Rooney's, a "tough" hangout which carries on drinking business behind closed doors after the one a.m. curfew. During the course of the story, in which the saloon is busted, Cork and Ruby connive their way out of arrest, and wind up at the door of the justice of the peace. Porter portrays the two not as perpetrators of crime and graft but as victims of a society which allows and accepts such action. The blame lies not on Cork for stabbing his rival but on the conditions which set up such relationships; it lies not on Fanny for offering the bribes, but on the policeman for accepting them. This design, however castigating, seems primarily intended not to make a social comment so much as to allow the story to develop in the way that it does. Porter's primary purpose here is to present a story of romance among the plebeians, flavored with the usual ironic twist of identity (since the girl's true identity is not revealed until the policeman tries to arrest Cork for the knifing), though in the telling the author slips in his own barbs for the conditions which produce this harsh lifestyle.

More grim and tragic is the outcome of "The Guilty Party," which concerns Kid Mullaly and his girl Liz. This story, featuring some narrative variations, is prefaced by a flashback depicting Liz as a child, forced to play in the street because her "redhaired, unshaven, untidy" father has no time for her (1441). Kid Mullaly accepts a bet that he will take Annie to the dance instead of his fiancee Liz. When the rejected girl learns of this betrayal, she bursts into the dance and drives a knife into the Kid's heart, then flees for the river to drown herself, while followed

the big city's biggest shame, its most ancient and rotten surviving canker, its pollution and disgrace, its blight and perversion, its forever infamy and guilt, fostered, unreproved and cherished, handed down from a long-ago century of the basest barbarity—the Hue and Cry. (1445)

The story ends with a dream of the narrator—a technique Porter often employed—set in the next world "where the judgments are going on" (1445), and a Special Terrestrial Officer reports the girl's case, with the conclusion that she had no defense. The court officer reprimands him, however, saying, "The guilty party you've got to look for in this case is a redhaired, unshaven, untidy man, sitting by the window reading, in his stocking feet, while his children play in the streets" (1446).

A story such as this one is certainly less sentimental than "The Venturers" or "Vanity and Some Sables," offering a more realistic picture of street gang life, and even seeming to deal harshly with a society which permits such conditions to exist. But Porter's purpose is effect, not reform. He uses these conditions as they are for background; they provide the stuff for his plots and the characters for his actions. As Current-Garcia points out, "If he could achieve now and then the incidental criticism of greedy landlords, miserly employers, or crooked public officials along with his entertainment, well and good; but the entertainment took precedence over everything else."[12]

Porter also allows conventional expectations to dictate the responses of these characters. A person would be expected to feel shame and remorse after committing such a murder as Liz commits, and she displays this guilt by drowning herself, though it's obvious that grief and despair also drive her to the river. Nevertheless, the reader is sympathetic towards her because she is truly not to blame for the conditions which have led to her action, and also because she displays the appropriate contrition. Her actions are to some extent justified, and this justification Porter seconds in his clever but manipulated ending.

Similar conventional reactions can be seen in the other street gang characters. Ruby—or Fanny—in "Past One At Rooney's," when her true identity is revealed to Cork, assumes that he will want nothing more to do with her, even though he is guilty of a crime himself: " 'I guess I might as well say good-by here,' she said dully. 'You won't want to see me again, of course' " (1613). Cork McManus counters with the conventional romantic reaction that he loves her in spite of her past, leading to a final romantic expectation whereby they presumably marry and both amend their wayward ways in favor of the straight life and the joys of love, thus reaffirming the restorative powers of love.

The plebeian character type, then, which encompasses the shopgirl and the clerk, the poor but happy young married couple, and the tough "East Side" kids, is based upon realistic conditions of poverty and deprivation. Accepting those conditions as they are, Porter creates stories in which the characters act within and influenced by those conditions. At times he romanticizes that world; at other times he implies criticism of it, often harsh. Sometimes his characters find happiness, while at other times they find only more misery or even death. These conditions encourage the reader's sympathy toward the characters and help to justify whatever otherwise unacceptable action they may take, such as murder or suicide. Appropriate remorse on the character's part also contributes to this alleviation of guilt.

VI

A final character type Porter develops in his city stories, the tramp, is also a product of conventional assumptions. Porter portrays him as the lone, battered figure on the park bench, the penniless poet, the down-and-out figure of former prosperity. The tramp may bum a dime for a cup of coffee, but still he is an individual of pride and principle; he is a ragged figure but he maintains a certain dignity; he dwells among the city's alleys and parks, but his thoughts are hopeful, even noble.

Perhaps the most well-known and beloved of Porter's tramps is Soapy of "The Cop and the Anthem," whose situation and outcome illustrate with sad humor the irony of fate. To spend the coming cold winter months in the warmth and comfort of the Island prison, Soapy cleverly devises numerous schemes to get himself arrested, from smashing a window to petty larceny. Failing pathetically in all of them, he finds himself pausing in front of a quaint old church on a quiet corner, from whence sweet organ music drifts, so stirring Soapy's soul that he vows to straighten up, get a job, and pay his own way. At that moment a policeman arrests him for vagrancy, and he receives a three-month sentence on the Island.

Who could respond with anything but irate sympathy to the nobility of Soapy, too proud to accept the humiliation of spirit wrought by charity, who recalls when hearing the anthem "the days when his life contained such things as mothers and roses and ambitions and friends and immaculate thoughts and collars" (41)?

Pride and principle are attributes of Porter's tramps. Sherrard Plumer, fallen painter of "A Madison Square Arabian Night," whom Chalmers invites in from the street, haughtily assesses his benefactor, assuming that an account of his hard luck is the price of a meal.

Stuffy Pete, in "Two Thanksgiving Day Gentlemen," is too proud and compassionate to tell The Old Gentleman, who for nine years has approached him at his Union Square park bench on Thanksgiving Day and taken him to eat a big dinner, that he has just eaten a tremendous meal provided unexpectedly by two annually benevolent old ladies. Instead, he accompanies The Old Gentleman, for whom this tradition is one of life's major occupations, and forces down a second meal, though afterwards he collapses from gluttony on the sidewalk outside. He is taken to a hospital, where an hour later The Old Gentleman is brought in too, suffering from starvation.

Even Prince Michael of the Electorate of Valleluna, a dope addict in "The Caliph, Cupid and the Clock," is noble in his ragged clothing and wretched shoes. He fancies himself to be a wealthy prince who has shunned the gold and jewels and pleasures of a rich station for the rags and dinginess of a park bench, preferring to study humanity "close to the unarmored, beating heart of the world" (77). Seated thus on his park bench next to a young man who is anxiously watching the great face of the clock in the tower, awaiting a sign of forgiveness from his mistress, the Prince convinces him to wait an extra half hour, promising if he does $100,000 and a palace on the Hudson as a wedding gift. The young man waits, and the long-awaited signal is given; the story ends with the Prince-bum asleep on the park bench, a fifty-dollar bill crumpled into his hand.

Such figures are pathetic in their deprivation, yet admirable in their unselfish and un-self-pitying means of coping with it. They embody the innate nobility of the human spirit in even the most down-and-out situation, undaunted by despair. This is an optimistic and hopeful view, for nothing "could be grimmer or more depressing in real life than the dope-pushing derelicts that haunt the park benches and Salvation Army soup kitchens."[13]

As mentioned earlier, the tramp is frequently a fallen aristocrat—or more accurately, a self-deposed aristocrat, unwilling to compromise his principles. Such is the case of Vallance and Kerner, both of whom refuse to establish class barriers by giving up women they loved, or at least entertained.

A similar question of principle has brought down young Murray and the Captain in "According To Their Lights" to the lowest ebb of fortune; "both had fallen from at least an intermediate Heaven of respectability and importance, and both were typical products of the monstrous and peculiar social curriculum of their overweening and bumptious civic alma mater" (1446). Both have fallen for reasons of moral compromise. When the Captain is approached by a diamond-studded fellow offering him five hundred dollars to testify against his former inspector, the Captain angrily drives him from the park saying, "I'm down and out; but I'm no traitor to a man that's been my friend" (1449). Murray calls him a fool, but when he is himself grabbed by a tall man who informs him that his uncle wants to restore him to favor on the condition that he marry a certain heiress, Murray abruptly refuses. Both place principle above money, whether five hundred dollars or two million; both act "according to their lights" (1451). They are no less noble in their downtrodden state than they were in their "respectable" ones; if anything, they are more so because of their admirable actions. In this respect, Porter's tramp satisfies conventional expectations; he does not allow poverty to erode his self-respect. In some cases, this integrity is rewarded, as when the aristocrat is restored to favor, having retained his values and his honor intact, in the tradition of the temptation trial. But even when he is not re-inherited, even when it appears that he is cut off forever from the life and luxury he is accustomed to, it is clear that the aristocrat-tramp will survive; the reader need have no concern for a character with his moral strength and his guiding standards of value.

Beneath their cultural coverings, all Porter's character types represent more universal figures, embodying traits and values common to the oldest literary characters. In her poverty-haunted straits, the shopgirl fills the role of the damsel-in-distress; she is Innocence in struggle with the forces of evil, which may be out to starve her, to stain her, or to otherwise ruin her. She, in turn, displays heroic strength, despite her trials. In his attempt to brighten his otherwise dull life with a ray of adventure, the habitual character resembles other seekers of adventure who reject the secure and the stable in quest of the unknown. Porter's character, however, usually does not stray far, returning ultimately to the ennui he sought to escape. The lover, of course, follows traditional patterns in his willingness to reform, to sacrifice, to forgive, even to die, for the person he or she loves. The aristocrat, in his refusal to conform to conventional values, asserts his individuality; he is a kind of rebel in his rejection of society and its empty standards, and such a character will typically sacrifice all his material possessions rather than compromise his moral principles. The plebeian is a kind of underdog, since he suffers from the deprivation which naturally comes with a society that can accommodate aristocracy. The tramp is also a kind of scapegoat, and a kind of outcast, having disrupted the values of conventional society with his obviously superior wisdom.

All of Porter's character types are marked by nobility in the form of principle, patience, or acceptance: the shopgirl who maintains a cheerful countenance and attitude despite her poverty; the domestic in the flat who accepts the routine existence of life; the lover who sacrifices for another's happiness; the aristocrat who seeks values other than money; the plebeian who plays the hand life has dealt him; the tramp who maintains his dignity above all. In this respect, they are all equal, all of one class, all of one type— the noble human character—despite the fact that social and economic standards stratify them. Even that separation is frequently dissolved, as Porter has the rich masquerade among the poor and "Pippalike, bestows upon the poverty-stricken clerk a day when he can become one with the rich."[14] The wealthy invite the tramps into their homes; the aristocrat leaves the sham of the country club for the honesty of the park.

Porter is not a crusader, but he is a humanitarian. He sees and presents in his stories the soul of the common man; and for him, all men are common. He not only watched "with meticulous carefulness all the idiosyncrasies of every sort of person with whom he came in contact, but he was further obsessed with a passionate interest in and sympathy with every type of man."[15] He concealed

behind laughing language a profound love for the great masses of people who are frequently called the little people. O. Henry himself probably never saw a little person unless he happened to see a midget.... People weren't little to O. Henry unless they *were*, but even then they were little only on the outside.[16]

The same types of individuals Porter wrote about are still around today. His characters, of course, were shaped by contemporary cultural forces, like the growing industrialism or the prominent business wealth. But although the times have changed, the people have not. The factory workers and the flat-dwellers (brick houses now, perhaps) are still to be found; the parks and city sidewalks are still crowded with homeless vagabonds and bag-ladies; the mass of our society is still fascinated with the lives of the wealthy, and indeed the vicarious participation in that envied lifestyle has become something of a modern industry.

Porter's character types are often criticized for shallowness and underdevelopment, for being "types" rather than individualized characters. To the extent that they are not fully rounded individuals, this criticism is certainly justified, and some reasons for this sketchy approach have already been suggested. It is true that Porter's characters are not particularly new or innovative, that they "come before us shaped, proportioned, weighted, exactly as the characters of Maupassant are shaped and proportioned."[17] Yet in view of their function as class representatives, their nature seems quite appropriate. While the reader may not remember Della as clearly as Carrie Meeber, or Ikey Schoenstein as well as Huckleberry Finn, the reader might remember the character type he or she represents, for it is the idea or abstraction of the type which really matters. The story "of *one* underpaid shop girl itself grips and holds you; the *idea* of *all* underpaid shop girls also enlarges and intensifies your thoughts about the whole problem dealt with, though you may not be as conscious of your thoughts on the subject as you are of your emotions."[18] Porter draws indistinct outlines of familiar characters who embody basic and universal human conflicts— conflicts between poverty and optimism, security and yearning, love and jealousy, temptation and honor. They are traditional character types presented in specific, contemporary, cultural habitats, and "why should not art be traditional as well as original?"[19]

Critic Cesare Pavese concurs in this analysis of the urban characters, viewing Porter's character abstractions in the context of his overall artistic purpose. Porter's heroes, writes Pavese, are naturally not monuments of psychology or pyres of passion: the language that describes them, the tone of the narration, the good-natured intimacy of the recollection, everything conspires to reduce their proportions, everything casts over O. Henry's events a faint shade of jest and of "philosophy"—which permits no creative luxury, in the usual sense of the term. In the act of conversing, O. Henry describes his types; he gives them a brush stroke and then he stops— looks at the listener—makes an observation on some related memory, winks with his eyes, gestures with his hands, changes the position of his cigar, gives another brush stroke. For it is not O. Henry's intention to describe such or such another character in the name of humanity; he tends simply to represent in the most direct and least pedantic way possible a memory of something indelible, curiously paradoxical. The principle that comprehends and unifies all his narrative art is just this, the knowing exposition of something intellectually unusual, bizarre, "queer."[20]

Through his power of literary transformation, Porter elevates the commonplace to the realm of importance, focusing our vision not on individual characters but on representatives of society's multifarious groups. His concern with the masses, with the everyday lives of everyday individuals—including the rich—is a hallmark of Porter's urban short stories, and his keen ability to capture the pleasures and sorrows, the hopes and frustrations, the values and morals of those lives, while spinning a clever and entertaining, sometimes haunting tale, attests to his artistic skills and to his ongoing popularity.

Conclusion

By virtue of his tremendous appeal, his singular style, and the prodigious amount of material he produced in his brief decade as an author, William Sydney Porter occupies a prominent position in American popular literature. Call him literary charlatan or call him short story genius; the man who called himself O. Henry earned his mark as a literary craftsman, making significant and lasting contributions to twentieth-century literature and influencing the development of the short story in America.

Whether that influence was for better or for worse is a matter of opinion, and judgments of Porter diverge sharply. Adamant admirers lavish praise upon him inordinately, while his harshest critics condemn him as shallow, cheap, flippant. "The time is coming, let us hope," predicted Stephen Leacock in 1916, "when the whole English-speaking world will recognize in O. Henry one of the great masters of modern literature,"[1] and Henry James Forman, writing in *North American Review* in 1908, commented, "It is idle to compare O. Henry with anybody. No talent could be more original or more delightful. The combination of technical excellence with whimsical, sparkling wit, abundant humour, and a fertile invention is so rare that the reader is content without comparisons."[2]

Pattee, on the other hand, while commending Porter's excellence in style and humor, ultimately accuses him of prostituting his art, suggesting that to rate him "as a maker of classics...is deplorable "[3] and that to offer him as a model for students undermines literature. "He moves us tremendously at times, but so does a narcotic," writes Pattee.[4] "That his work has in it oases of beauty, that he has moments when he shows himself possessed of surprising powers, that he is original even to a startling degree, only emphasizes the tragedy of his literary career. His undoubted powers he surrendered deliberately to Momus."[5]

Similar disparity marks the discussions of Porter's contributions to American literature. That he did indeed affect the genre is undisputed, but assessments of that influence range from "remarkable" to "alarming." It seems a rather fitting irony that the very sort of contrariety marking Porter's life and art also pervades the response and the criticism his work generates.

Porter's most obvious and significant legacy to the short story is the technique of plot design. His deft handiwork, seemingly so effortless, impelled hordes of imitators to attempt reproductions. "More than anyone else he helped to turn the tide of short fiction in the direction of manner."[6] During the decade following Porter's death, magazine fiction became dominated by an obsession with form, especially the trick ending, and the first dozen or so annual collections of *O. Henry Prize Stories*, initiated in 1919, were also characterized by "good craftsmanship" above all else.[7]

These formulaic patterns, especially the unexpected endings, comprise the heart of Porter's stories, his style, and his popularity as well. But Porter's endings "are not merely a surprise or contrary to expectation, they appear in a sort of lateral way [sic]...; and it is only then that the reader realizes that certain details here and there had hinted at the possibility of such an ending."[8]

Furthermore, Porter's mechanical approach to structuring fiction encouraged the proliferation of short story handbooks that began with the century. The decipherment of plot structures explored in Chapter Four illustrates how the stories can be stripped to their bare bones, prompting the assumption that, armed with these patterns, one can easily rebuild other stories just as excellent. The fallacy of that logic is obvious, but it did not deter eager novices. In the century's opening years, "short story art in America began to be exploited as if it were an exact science," and this decade became "the era of the short-story handbook,"[9] with its sure-fire rules for constructing a piece of fiction.

Obviously, Porter's art consists of far more than plot contrivance, as any attempt at imitation quickly reveals, but though Porter's immediate influence upon this technique waned after another decade, he is still generally associated with the "formula story." Just as Edgar Allan Poe's name is indelibly woven to the tale of terror, so the name of O. Henry conjures up the clever, surprise-ending story. Like Poe, he is concerned primarily with effect; he perceives the culmination from the beginning and focuses all elements towards that end, executing his literary *coup de grace* with finesse and efficiency.

> It would seem that the story is ended, instead of begun; that the close of tragedy and the climax of a romance have covered the ground of interest; but, to the more curious reader it shall be some slight instruction to trace the close threads that underlie the ingenuous web of circumstances. (552)

Porter's impress upon popular literature manifests itself in other areas as well. He infused the language of storytelling with a vibrant originality, scattering fresh phrases, piquant metaphors, and startling exaggerations as freely and profusely as a spring sower, reeling off dialect and local description with acumen, and introducing a peculiar but original discursive style that irritates some and delights others, prompting his biographer to conclude that the "short story in 1904 and 1905 developed a new flexibility, established new means of communication between literature and life, and, as a mirror of certain aspects of American society, attained a fidelity and an adequacy never before achieved."[10] Such a critique seems justified for a man who could begin a story this way: "Inexorably Sam Galloway saddled his pony" (811). Or this: "When the forefinger of twilight begins to smudge the clear-drawn lines of the Big City there is inaugurated an hour devoted to one of the most melancholy sights of urban life" (839). One critic cites Porter's variety of euphemism as his most prominent mannerism. "John Phoenix invented the device but O. Henry gave it circulation. So completely did the trick take possession of him that one may denominate it almost as a *cliché*, the trademark of O. Henry."[11]

Porter's brand of humor, too, is a distinct contribution to this American tradition. As "the twentieth century successor of John Phoenix and Artemus Ward,"[12] Porter is sly, dry-witted, whimsical, a caricaturist by nature, a punster and practical joker, a vaudevillian who shuffles words to evoke laughter: "She had a gamut that I estimate at about eight inches on the piano; and her runs and trills sounded like the clothes bubbling in your grandmother's iron wash-pot. Believe that she must have been beautiful when I tell you that it sounded like music to us" (806). His humor flashes as rapidly as his language, often resulting from those rhetorical concoctions.

"Images, turns, strange conceits, fantastic foolishness pour in upon him like a flood. He is gay, irresponsible, impudent, hoaxing; no writer in the language seems clever immediately after one has been reading O. Henry."[13]

Much has been made of Porter's "humanization" and "socialization" of the short story, an aspect which is also linked to his place in realism. Porter's biographer argues that the writer was more concerned with humanity than with plot intrigue in his art:

It is O. Henry's distinction that he has enlarged the area of the American short story by enriching and diversifying its social themes. In his hands the short story has become the organ of a social consciousness more varied and multiform than it had ever expressed before.... An instant responsiveness to the humor or the pathos or the mere human interest of men and women playing their part in the drama of life was always his distinguishing characteristic.... Beneath the power to observe and the skill to reproduce lay a passionate interest in social phenomena which with him no other interest ever equalled or even threatened to replace.[14]

That Porter felt a deep and sincere passion for people, particularly the displaced and defeated, is unquestionable, and that the ebb and flow of their lives stirred his curiosity and his writer's instinct is apparent in his tales. He is astute at perceiving human motives and desires. But it is also clear that he constantly mined for "an idea," a point on which his story could turn, preferably paradoxical. Humanity lies at the heart of "The Cop and the Anthem," for example, but so does the irony of Soapy's final conversion.

On the whole, Porter's work is not strongly enough committed to exposure of the sordid side of life to be considered realism— at least, not of the calibre of a Norris, Crane, or Sinclair. He does contribute realistic details, settings, and situations, and he does display a preoccupation with lives and dilemmas of the down-and-out. But still, effect is his overriding concern and his chief hallmark, and effect is vital to the very nature of O. Henryism.

Besides, Porter was always too much the reticent observer ever to be the alacritous reformer, even if his stories did prompt Theodore Roosevelt's progressive measures for shopgirls.[15] In his life, in his personality, and in his work, Porter preferred always to remain on the sidelines:

He was no indiscriminate lover of the human race, swollen to quick tears and tenderness at the mere proximity of a crowd. He was not even a hail fellow.... His whole life was a spectatorship.... His work alone carries the proof that he was a spectator. Few workers could have mastered the details of so many crafts as he learned how to use, in fiction, by his observant loafing. Moreover,...almost all his stories have at least one end in the street or some public place.... And finally, there was in his temper a certain balance arising out of a philosophy which, whether natural or deliberate, is invariably a detached philosophy, a spectator's reading of life.[16]

One other feature which should be noted as part of Porter's legacy to popular literature is his spirit of romance, a quality which flowers fully in his prismatic vision of New York City: its clamoring, swarming crowds, its endless streets and sights, its promise of wondrous occurrences at any moment, on any corner.

In the big city the twin spirits Romance and Adventure are always abroad seeking worthy wooers. As we roam the streets they slyly peep at us and challenge us in twenty different guises. Without knowing why, we look up suddenly to see in a window a face that seems to belong to our gallery of intimate portraits; in a sleeping thoroughfare we hear a cry of agony and fear coming from an empty and shuttered house; instead of at our familiar curb a cab-driver deposits us before a strange door, which one, with a smile, opens for us and bids to enter; a slip of paper, written upon, flutters down to our feet from the high lattices of Chance; we exchange glances of instantaneous hate, affection, and fear with hurrying strangers in the passing crowds; a sudden souse of rain—and our umbrella may be sheltering the daughter of the Full Moon and first cousin of the Sidereal System; at every corner handkerchiefs drop, fingers beckon, eyes besiege, and the lost, the lonely, the rapturous, the mysterious, the perilous changing clues of adventure are slipped into our fingers. (63)

What strange and marvelous dreams he weaves, this Scheherazade of the metropolis! His stories recall those old favorites of his, *The Arabian Nights*, and indeed Porter is fashioning his own wonder tales out of an ancient tradition of romance, once again infusing them with his magical vision to produce new forms that are both popular and satisfying.

This quality of fulfillment, of course, lies at the very heart of popular romance. It is the super-natural providence of the world of fiction, and the changes which have come over the fashions in heroes and manners have not essentially altered it.... Deity, saint, coincidence,—something must furnish the element of wonder and the desired miracle. One should not be misled by the fact that new names have been given to the mysterious agent. Named or nameless, it has existed and exists to accomplish in art the defeated aspirations of reality. It is O. Henry's most powerful aid, brilliant in his endings, everywhere pervasive.[17]

It is the blending of all these distinctive qualities with an array of traditional popular forms that marks Porter as a popular artist. Though his peculiar literary manner, so well-suited to the age in which he lived and wrote, is no longer in vogue, he still bears a curious affinity to our contemporary society. Today's world is a kaleidoscope of types, some the same as in Porter's time—the businessman, the secretary, the lover, the tramp—and some of a more modern ilk: the corporate executive, the New Woman, and the entrepreneur, for example, or the hippies, the yuppies, the punkers, the joggers. What might a modern Porter make of this harried society teeming with people who wear their identities on their t-shirts, their cars, and their credit cards? Most of us, at some point, have muttered those words which crop up so often in Porter's tales: "You know the type."

Furthermore, formula has become predominant in modern literature and entertainment—disturbingly so. Its influence on television, music, movies, novels, and magazines is staggering—not to mention the other dimensions of society such as shopping malls and fast food restaurants. Unfortunately, most of this output abuses formula, rarely exhibiting that ingredient of originality which distinguishes creative spirits like Porter.

His style of storytelling is unique, securely ensconced in the chronicles of American popular literature, and his influence upon the short story genre, whether considered favorable or unfortunate, is undeniable. He is, in fact, a rather pivotal figure in the evolution of the genre, for

he wrote at the end of a tradition of short fiction, headed by Irving and Poe, and in which he benefited from a century of experiment and achievement.... O. Henry is the last in a line of self-conscious practitioners of an art, all master craftsmen well initiated into its mysteries. He can thus deconstruct, in the fashionable phrase of our day, the dead and dying forms surrounding him. Out of that deconstruction...he supplies his own boneyard of material for the creation of new formal possibilities in literary art.[18]

The artistic phoenix which Porter resurrected is a short story distinctly his own, bearing his signature as clearly as does a Chaplin performance or a Hitchcock movie. Though critic Leslie Fiedler suggests that "popular art is lacking in qualities which I have called 'signature elements,' " Porter's individualism implies just the opposite.[19] His work is the sum of his particular characteristics and qualities, a carefully constructed unit whose success depends upon this combination of elements rather than solely upon story action or characterization. The O. Henryism is produced by placing a certain character type within a certain plot pattern, then getting to the point of it through a maze of peculiar sentence structures, allusions, and plot manipulations, with clues to the surprise ending subtly woven into the exposition.

In the long run, of course, as with any artist, one's response to and judgment of Porter is subjective and, to some extent, results from or reflects an attitude toward popular literature in general. For Porter is first and foremost a popular artist, and his work bears the distinguishing characteristics of that genre: it aims to accommodate a majority of readers, it is easily comprehended, and it has achieved widespread distribution. Furthermore, it is familiar: Porter is clearly a formulaic writer, and his heavy dependance upon formula often—to some minds, at least—disparages his identity as a creative artist. For the quality and value of formulaic literature, and in fact of all popular literature, is a subject of ongoing debate among critics, and since art by its very nature defies any final, restrictive definition, no ultimate, infallible judgment can ever be rendered. But regardless of whether one views formulaic literature as mechanical prostitution or as a means to creativity, one aspect of it cannot be overlooked or denied: its popular appeal. Popular literature and formula stories, whether in the form of books, movies, or television shows, have continually dominated public taste, enjoying wide appeal among people of all ages and types. As Cawelti points out, "Even scholars and critics professionally dedicated to the serious study of artistic masterpieces often spend their off-hours following a detective's ritual pursuit of a murderer or watching one of television's spy teams carry through its dangerous mission."[20]

The very basis of formula, the careful tension between repetition and innovation, is an intrinsic element of the natural world and of human existence; by extension, it is fundamental to human literature. The fairy tales and myths are formula stories, filled with monsters, heroes, and other "types," built on well-known patterns in which good generally triumphs over evil. Children hearing stories of the wondrous and fantastic "clutch at the security of the familiar," demanding to hear the same old story again and again, while adults "continue to find a special delight in familiar stories" that fulfill their expectations.[21]

For readers, then, formula stories can be extremely satisfying and comforting. For Porter, formula opens the door to creativity; it is vital to his art. Building on conventional plot structures familiar to readers and employing recognizable character types, Porter weaves a style that is fresh and original, a compilation of diverse elements: his plots, characters, and snappy endings, of course; his story openings which, like his closings, are drawn from a stock file of forms such as anecdotal, expository, or chatty; his calculated digressions (which were probably ploys to fill valuable copy inches); his heavy use of Biblical and classical allusions; and his ingenious manipulation of language, evident in precise metaphors, extended circumlocutions, unbalanced phrases, unimaginable dialogue, and extraordinary vocabulary. All these characteristics combine to produce the overall effect that is the O. Henry story, and this effect lies at the heart of his popularity.

To some readers, this effect seems disreputable and tawdry, Porter's literary sleights-of-hand being little more than trickery; to others, the effect is masterful. Russian readers, for example, appreciate the "dexterity of construction, cleverness of plot situations and dénouements, compactness and swiftness of action,"[22] qualities lacking in their own literature. It may be true that O. Henry stressed manner at the expense of matter, "that he loved effect too much and truth too little," but that is "essential to writing good stories."[23] Besides, the author is honest and straight- forward about his structural tricks: "The art of narrative consists in concealing from your audience everything it wants to know until after you expose your favorite opinions on topics foreign to the subject."[24]

Porter is no James Joyce or William Faulkner. He does not aim to be and should not be judged by the same criteria. He is a serious and original artist, yet he can also be a trickster. Even the most faithful O. Henry fans must concede his weaknesses and acknowledge that his stature does not rank among the greatest of literary artists. Porter himself recognized this; a few months before his death, he fretted,. "I want to get at something bigger. What I have done is child's play to what I can do, to what I know it is in me to do."[25]

But what he *did* do, he did well. Working within the conventional confines of his material, Porter produced an original form of art. He is a formulaic writer, yet he stands apart from and above those faceless manufacturers of lifeless formulaic material. The difference is the sort suggested by Wallace Stegner between "the writer of serious fiction and the writer of escape entertainment." One is an artist, the other a craftsman. "The one has the privilege and the faculty of original design; the other does not. The man who works from blueprints is a thoroughly respectable character but he is of another order from the man who makes the blueprints in the first place."[26]

Porter is both craftsman and artist. He borrows blueprints, and he works from his own as well; he uses characters whose lineage reaches far back in time, yet he clothes them in garbs of his own cloth; he speaks with clichés and metaphors but they seem to be uttered for the first time. Porter is a literary Rumplestiltskin, spinning his golden tales from the straw and flax of everyday fields. The treasures he concocted won him success, admiration, and— for a few stories, at least—immortality. His work defies the implication that popular literature is distinguishable from high literature as a "certain kind of book whose author is forgotten though the work is remembered,"[27] such as Sherlock Holmes and Tarzan, with their more obscure creators Arthur Conan Doyle and Edgar Rice Burroughs.

For who will remember "The Gift of the Magi" without remembering O. Henry? Who could envision the figure of the shopgirl or the tramp without glimpsing the shadow of their creator hovering in the background? Some might even recall the basic plot of the story but forget its title, yet know unmistakably that it is an O. Henry story. Indeed, if there is anything forgettable about Porter's stories, it is—as many critics have pointed out—the titles, but certainly not the author. An O. Henry tale, by its very nature, is intrinsically associated with its author, for the author's distinctive style is what makes it remembered in the first place. Take away the O. Henryism of the story and you take away the very soul of the story. Indeed, a reader even vaguely familiar with the author might read a story he has never before seen and identify it as O. Henry's on the basis of the surprise ending or some other characteristic mark.

It is as a New York writer that Porter became, and remains, most famous, and his urban stories comprise a form of popular art that is both singular and formulaic. In one respect, it is self-contained: his plot structures repeat themselves consistently, with variations upon certain defined patterns, and his characters are types which appear repeatedly throughout his stories, displaying only minor individual characteristics. In another respect, however, his art touches upon the broader, more universal aspects of formula, as he builds plots and sketches characters upon models long familiar in literature.

Since Porter produced material to meet a weekly deadline, working against the standard of time rather than artistic merit, it was perhaps inevitable that his stories would be standardized; such standardization certainly is one ingredient of his popularity. But Porter imbued this standardization with cultural and individual elements which offered his audience the opportunity to relate to the stories and to be entertained by them simultaneously. Drawing upon plot structures and character types which reflect conventional beliefs and attitudes, merging them with cultural factors and stylistic innovations. Porter created a short story form which was entertaining, suspenseful, and satisfying, providing an acceptable balance of the familiar and the unfamiliar. That balance is the basis of formula, and the basis of the formulaic art of Porter's urban short stories.

Notes

Introduction

[1] Al Jennings, *Through the Shadows with O. Henry* (N.Y.: H.K. Fly Co., 1921), p. 280.

[2] Stephen Leacock, "The Amazing Genius of O. Henry," in Leacock's *Essays and Literary Studies* (N.Y.: John Lane Co., 1916), pp. 246-47.

[3] Jennings, p. 280.

[4] "Chronicle and Comment," *The Bookman*, July 1908, p. 436.

[5] Quoted in George MacAdam, "O. Henry's Only Autobiographia," in *O. Henry Papers: Containing Some Sketches of His Life Together With An Alphabetical Index to His Complete Works*, rev. ed. (Garden City, N.Y.: Doubleday, Doran & Co., Inc., n.d.; Folcroft Library Eds., 1971), p. 21.

[6] Joseph Campbell, *The Hero With A Thousand Faces*, vol. 17 of Bollingen Series (Princeton, N.J.: Princeton Univ. Press, 1949), p. 4.

[7] John C. Cawelti, *Adventure, Mystery, and Romance* (Chicago: Univ. of Chicago Press, 1976), p. 1.

[8] Gilbert Seldes, "The People and the Arts," in Bernard Rosenberg and David Manning White, eds., *Mass Culture: The Popular Arts in America* (Glencoe, Ill,: The Free Press, 1957), p. 79.

[9] Cawelti, p. 1.

[10] Quoted in John Updike, "The Artist and His Audience," *The New York Review of Books*, 18 July 1985, p. 14.

Chapter One

[1] Van Wyck Brooks, *The Confident Years, 1885-1915* (N.Y.: E.P. Dutton & Co., 1952), p. 267.

[2] C. Alphonso Smith, *O. Henry Biography* (N.Y.: Doubleday, 1916), p. 3.

[3] Ibid., p. 4.

[4] Tom Tate quoted by Arthur W. Page in "Little Pictures of O. Henry," *The Bookman*, 37 (June 1913): 385.

[5] Quoted in MacAdam, "O. Henry's Only Autobiographia," pp. 17-18.

[6] E. Hudson Long, *O. Henry: The Man and His Work* (Phila.: Univ. of Pa. Press, 1949), p. 18.

[7] Ibid., p. 18.

[8] Smith, p. 85.

[9] Long, p. 19.

[10] Ibid., p. 19.

[11] Smith, p. 86.

[12]Quoted by Arthur W. Page, "Little Pictures," pp. 386-87.

[13]Smith, p. 248.

[14]Smith, p. 173.

[15]Seth Moyle, *My Friend O. Henry* (N.Y.: H.K. Fly Co., 1914), p. 30.

[16]Long, pp. 25-26.

[17]Arthur W. Page, "Little Pictures of O. Henry," *The Bookman*, 37 (July 1913): 498.

[18]Smith, p. 112.

[19]Long, p. 131.

[20]Smith, pp. 115-16.

[21]Paul Aubrey Tracy, *A Closer Look at O. Henry's Rolling Stone* (Master's Thesis, Univ. of Texas, 1949), quoted in Frank Luther Mott, *A History of American Magazines, Vol. IV: 1885-1905* (Cambridge, MA.: Harvard Univ. Press, 1957), p. 670.

[22]Page, 37 (July 1913): 506.

[23]Mott, p. 666.

[24]William Sydney Porter, *Rolling Stone*, 2 (Sept. 8, 1894): 2; quoted by Mott, p. 667.

[25]Quoted in MacAdam, p. 18.

[26]Smith, p. 137.

[27]Ibid., p. 145.

[28]Ibid., p. 143.

[29]Ibid., p. 148.

[30]Ibid., p. 148.

[31]Jennings, pp. 134-35.

[32]Jennings, pp. 244-47.

[33]Gerald Langford, *Alias O. Henry* (N.Y.: Macmillan, 1957), p. 137.

[34]Smith, p. 155.

[35]Kent Bales, "O. Henry," in A. Walton Litz, editor-in-chief, *American Writers*, Supp. II, Part I: *W.H. Auden to O. Henry* (N.Y.: Charles Scribner's Sons, 1981), p. 392.

[36]Jennings, p. 222.

[37]Smith, pp. 166-67.

[38]Foster Rhea Dulles, *The United States Since 1865* (Ann Arbor, MI: Univ. of Mich. Press, 1959), p. 178.

[39]Alfred Kazin, *On Native Grounds* (N.Y.: Harcourt Brace Jovanovich, 1942), pp. 51, 53.

[40]Fred Lewis Pattee, *The New American Literature*, 1890-1930 (N.Y.: The Century Co., 1930), p. 3.

[41]Ibid., p. 103.

[42]Mott, p. 1.

[43]Kazin, p. 53.

[44]Pattee, p. 167.

[45]Brooks, p. 267.

[46]Robert H. Davis and Arthur B. Maurice, *The Caliph of Bagdad* (N.Y.: n.p., 1931), p. 174.

[47]Smith, p. 173.

[48]Dulles, p. 89.

[49]Quentin Reynolds, *The Fiction Factory or From Pulp Row to Quality Street* (N.Y.: Random House, 1955), p. 3.

[50]Ibid., pp. 123, 125.

[51]Ibid., p. 125.

[52]T.S. Eliot, quoted in Ernest Van Den Haag, "Of Happiness and Despair We Have No Measure," in Rosenberg and White, eds., *Mass Culture*, p. 505.

[53]Reynolds, p. 125.

[54]Mott, p. 3.

[55]Pattee, p. 313.

[56]Dulles, p. 107.

[57]Pattee, p. 313.

[58]Pattee, pp. 49, 57.

[59]Mott, p. 113.

[60]Reynolds, p. 131.

[61]Brooks, p. 266.

[62]Russel Nye, *The Unembarrassed Muse: The Popular Arts in America* (N.Y.: The Dial Press, 1970), p. 3.

[63]Quoted in Reynolds, p. 142.

[64]Pattee, pp. 160, 162.

[65]Pattee, p. 3.

[66]Bales, p. 386.

[67]Pattee, pp. 321-22.

[68]Pattee, p. 167.

Chapter Two

[1]William Saroyan, "Oh What A Man Was O. Henry," *Kenyon Review*, 29 (November 1967): 672.

[2]Quoted in Fred Lewis Pattee, *The Development of the American Short Story* (N.Y.: Harper, 1923), p. 361.

[3]"A Yankee Maupassant," in O. Henry, *Waifs and Strays* (Garden City, N.Y.: Doubleday, Page & Co., 1919), pp. 272-73.

[4]Bales, p. 396.

[5]"A Yankee Maupassant," pp. 275-76.

[6]"O. Henry's Full House" was released in 1952 by Twentieth Century Fox. Filmed in black & white, it was directed by Henry Koster, Henry Hathaway, Jean Negulesco, and Henry King, and produced by Andre Hakim. The screenplays were written by Lamar Trotti, Richard Breen, Ivan Goff, Ben Roberts, and Walter Bullock, and the stars included Charles Laughton, Marilyn Monroe, Dale Robertson, Richard Widmark, Anne Baxter, Jean Peters, Fred Allen, and Farley Granger.

[7]Bosley Crowther, "O. Henry," review of "O. Henry's Full House," *New York Times*, 17 October 1952, p. 33, col. 1.

[8]Nye, p. 4.

⁹A detailed examination of all these elements would be too extensive for the purpose of this study and so is not included here.

¹⁰Brooks, p. 265.

¹¹An entertaining and informative account of this mass magazine production is provided in Reynolds' history of the Smith & Street Publishing Co. in *The Fiction Factory*.

¹²Pattee, *Development*, p. 361.

¹³Stuart Hall and Paddy Whannel, *The Popular Arts* (London: Hutchinson Educational Ltd. [The Anchor Press]. 1964), pp. 68-69.

¹⁴Ibid., p. 69.

¹⁵The *auteur* theory was developed by a loosely knit group of film critics writing for *Cahiers du Cinéma* in France in the mid-fifties, who were interested in analyzing the work of American filmmakers. Among the studies which offer valuable discussions of this theory are Wollen's *Signs and Meaning in the Cinema*, Sarris' *The American Cinema*, and Arthur Knight's *The Liveliest Art* (N.Y.: Macmillan, 1957; rev. ed. 1978).

¹⁶John C. Cawelti, "Notes Toward An Aesthetic of Popular Culture," in Ray B. Browne, ed., *Popular Culture and the Expanding Consciousness* (N.Y.: John Wiley & Sons, Inc., 1973), p. 55.

¹⁷Peter Wollen, *Signs and Meaning in the Cinema* (London: Martin Secker & Warburg, Ltd., 1969), p. 74.

¹⁸Wollen, p. 77.

¹⁹Andrew Sarris, *The American Cinema* (N.Y.: E.P. Dutton, 1968), p. 31.

²⁰Sarris, p. 36.

²¹Cawelti, "Notes," p. 55.

²²Ibid., p. 58.

²³Cawelti, *Adventure*, p. 5.

²⁴John C. Cawelti, "The Concept of Formula in the Study of Popular Literature," *Journal of Popular Culture*, 3 (1969): 385.

²⁵Ibid., 385.

²⁶Cawelti, *Adventure*, p. 5.

²⁷Ibid., p. 5.

²⁸Boris M. Ejxenbaum, *O. Henry and the Theory of the Short Story*, tr. I.R. Titunik, no. 1 in Michigan Slavic Contributions, gen. ed. L. Matejka (Ann Arbor: Univ. of Mich., 1968), p. 3.

²⁹Cawelti, *Adventure*, p. 6.

³⁰Ibid., p. 6.

³¹Cawelti, "Concept," 386.

Chapter Three

¹James Douglas, "An English Reaction to O. Henry," *Greensboro Daily News*, 15 April 1917, p. 4.

²Blanche Williams, *A Handbook on Story Writing* (N.Y.: Dodd, Mead, & Co., 1920), p. 74.

³William Sydney Porter (O. Henry), *The Complete Works of O. Henry*, fore. Harry Hansen (Garden City, N.Y.: Doubleday, 1953), p. 7. All the quotations from Porter's stories will be cited from this edition of his works and will be noted by page number, within parentheses, in the text of this book.

⁴Williams, p. 102.

⁵This story is often cited in discussions of Porter's style, and judgment of it has been divided. Stephen Leacock, for example, argues, "It shows O. Henry at his best as a master of that supreme pathos that springs...from the fundamental things of life itself. In the sheer art of narration, there is nothing done by Maupassant that surpasses" it (Leacock, p. 189). Brooks and Warren, on the other hand, probably the harshest critics, accuse Porter of cheap sentimentality, of resorting to trickery "to compensate for defects within the body of the story itself." The motivation for the ending, they argue, is too weak (Cleanth Brooks and Robert Penn Warren, *Understanding Fiction*, 2nd ed. [N.Y.: Appleton-Century-Crofts, Inc., 1959; orig. pub. 1943], pp. 95-98). Kent Bales counters this argument by suggesting that if "suicide is...often imprecisely motivated, that [if] the suicide's mind is often tired and confused...then O. Henry's 'motivation' becomes more satisfyingly realistic and the ending more nearly meaningful" (Bales, p. 398).

⁶Williams, pp. 265-66.

⁷This meeting of assumed identity and true identity could be seen as a union also. However, I present it as an exchange because the two identities do not merge; one is put aside when the other is taken on. Of course, since both identities center in one character, it can be argued that there is an intrinsic union.

⁸Williams, p. 73.

⁹Foster Harris, *The Basic Patterns of Plot* (Norman, Okla.: Univ. of Okla. Press, 1959), p. 36.

¹⁰Harris, p. 38.

¹¹Smith, p. 208.

¹²Cawelti, *Adventure*, p. 16.

¹³Quoted in Cawelti, *Adventure*, p. 16.

¹⁴Cawelti, *Adventure*, p. 16.

Chapter Four

¹Eugene Current-Garcia, *O. Henry* (N.Y.: Twayne Publishers, Inc., 1965), p. 99.

²Smith, pp. 205-06.

³Harry Hansen, ed., *The Pocket Book of O. Henry Stories* (N.Y.: Pocket Books, Inc., 1956), p. xi.

⁴Smith, p. 233.

⁵Current-Garcia suggests a similar approach in his book. He mentions three bases on which classification might be founded: the kinds of activities the characters engage in; the problems of adjustment they face; and the themes of the stories themselves.

⁶Stuart P.B. Mais, *From Shakespeare to O. Henry: Studies in Literature* (N.Y.: Dodd, Mead & Co., 1923), p. 308.

⁷Current-Garcia, p. 108.

⁸Kris Kristofferson, "Lovin' Arms."

⁹Edward J. O'Brien, *The Short Story Case Book* (N.Y.: Farrar & Rinehart, Inc., 1935), p. 198.

¹⁰Paul Simon, "Richard Cory," *Sounds of Silence* (Eclectic Music Co., Columbia Records, 1965).

¹¹Current-Garcia, p. 109.

¹²Ibid., p. 122.

¹³Ibid., p. 113.

¹⁴Mais, p. 305.

¹⁵Ibid., p. 305.

¹⁶Saroyan, 672.

¹⁷Virginia Woolf, "An Essay in Criticism," in *Granite and Rainbow* (N.Y.: Harcourt, Brace & Co., 1958), p. 86. Orig. publ. in *New York Herald Tribune*, 9 October 1927.

¹⁸Thomas H. Uzzell, *Narrative Technique: A Practical Course in Literary Psychology* (N.Y.: Harcourt, Brace & Co., 1923), p. 111.

¹⁹Woolf, p. 87.

²⁰Cesare Pavese, "O. Henry; or, The Literary Trick," in *American Literature: Essays and Opinions*, tr. Edwin Fussell (Berkeley, CA: Univ. of Calif. Press, 1970), p. 87.

Conclusion

¹Leacock, p. 247.

²Henry James Forman, "O. Henry's Short Stories," *North American Review*, (May 1908): 781.

³Pattee, *Sidelights*, p. 39.

⁴Ibid., p. 38.

⁵Ibid., p. 27.

⁶Pattee, *New American Literature*, p. 177.

⁷Ibid., p. 178.

⁸Ejxenbaum, p. 21.

⁹Pattee, *Development*, p. 364.

¹⁰Smith, p. 200.

¹¹Pattee, *New American Literature*, p. 170.

¹²Ibid., p. 167.

¹³Carl Van Doren, "O. Henry," *Texas Review*, 2 (January 1917): 252.

¹⁴Smith, pp. 204-05.

¹⁵Roosevelt said, "The reforms that I attempted in behalf of the shopgirls of New York were suggested by the stories of O. Henry." Quoted by Ejxenbaum, p. 57.

¹⁶Van Doren, 255-56.

¹⁷Ibid., 254.

¹⁸Bales, p. 399.

[19]Leslie Fiedler, "Giving the Devil His Due," *Journal of Popular Culture*, 12 (1979): 199.

[20]Cawelti, *Adventure*, p. 1.

[21]Ibid., p. 1.

[22]Ejxenbaum, p. 3.

[23]Ejxenbaum quoted by Bales, p. 398.

[24]William Sydney Porter, *Cabbages and Kings*, quoted in Cesare Pavese, "O. Henry; or, The Literary Trick," p. 80.

[25]Smith, p. 248.

[26]Wallace Stegner, *The Writer in America* (n.p.: Hokuseido Press, 1951), p. 3.

[27]Fiedler, 200.

Bibliography

Bales, Kent. "O. Henry." In A. Walton Litz, editor-in-chief, *American Writers*, Supp. II, Part I: *W.H. Auden to O. Henry.* N.Y.: Charles Scribner's Sons, 1981, pp. 385-412.

Brooks, Van Wyck. *The Confident Years, 1885-1915.* N.Y.: E.P. Dutton & Co., 1952.

Brooks, Cleanth, and Robert Penn Warren. *Understanding Fiction.* 2nd ed. N.Y.: Appleton-Century-Crofts, Inc., 1959. Orig. publ. 1943.

Campbell, Joseph. *The Hero With A Thousand Faces.* Vol. 17 of Bollingen Series. Princeton, N.J.: Princeton Univ. Press, 1949.

Cawelti, John C. *Adventure, Mystery, and Romance.* Chicago: Univ. of Chicago Press, 1976.

———. ."The Concept of Formula in the Study of Popular Literature." *Journal of Popular Culture*, 3 (1969): 381-90.

———. ."Notes Toward An Aesthetic of Popular Culture." In Ray B. Browne, ed. *Popular Culture and the Expanding Consciousness.* N.Y.: John Wiley & Sons, Inc., 1973, pp. 45-59. Orig. publ in *Journal of Popular Culture*, 5 (Fall 1971): 255-68.

"Chronicle and Comment." *The Bookman*, July 1908, p. 436.

Crowther, Bosley, "O. Henry." Review of "O. Henry's Full House." *New York Times*, 17 October 1952, p. 33, col. 1.

Current-Garcia, Eugene, *O. Henry (William Sydney Porter).* N.Y.: Twayne Publishers, Inc., 1965.

Davis, Robert H., and Arthur B. Maurice. *The Caliph of Bagdad.* N.Y.: n.p., 1931.

Douglas, James. "An English Reaction to O. Henry." *Greensboro Daily News*, 15 April 1917, p. 4.

Dulles, Foster Rhea. *The United States Since 1865.* Ann Arbor, MI: Univ. of Mich. Press, 1959.

Ejxenbaum, Boris M. *O. Henry and the Theory of the Short Story.* Tr. I.R. Titunik. No. 1 in Michigan Slavic Contributions, Gen. ed. L. Matejka. Ann Arbor, MI: Univ. of Mich., 1968.

Fiedler, Leslie. "Giving The Devil His Due." *Journal of Popular Culture*, 12 (1979): 197-207.

Forman, Henry James. "O. Henry's Short Stories." *North American Review*, May 1908, p. 781.

Hall, Stuart, and Paddy Whannel. *The Popular Arts.* London: Hutchinson Educational Ltd. (The Anchor Press), 1964.

Hansen, Harry, ed. *The Pocket Book of O. Henry Stories*. N.Y.: Pocket Books, Inc., 1956.

Harris, Foster. *The Basic Patterns of Plot*. Norman, Okla.: Univ. of Okla. Press, 1959.

Jennings, Al. *Through the Shadows with O. Henry*. N.Y.: H.K. Fly Co., 1921.

Kazin, Alfred. *On Native Grounds*. N.Y.: Harcourt Brace Jovanovich, 1942.

Kristofferson Kris. "Lovin' Arms."

Langford, Gerald. *Alias O. Henry: A Biography of William Sidney Porter*. N.Y. Macmillan, 1957.

Leacock, Stephen. "The Amazing Genius of O. Henry." In Stephen Leacock. *Essays and Literary Studies*. N.Y.: John Lane Co., 1916, pp. 246-47.

Long, E. Hudson. *O. Henry: The Man and His Work*. Phila.: Univ. of Pa. Press, 1949.

MacAdam, George. "O. Henry's Only Autobiographia." In *O. Henry Papers: Containing Some Sketches of His Life Together With An Alphabetical Index to His Complete Works*. Rev. ed. Garden City, N.Y. Doubleday, Doran & Co., n.d. Folcroft Library Eds., 1971.

Mais, Stuart P.B. *From Shakespeare to O. Henry: Studies in Literature*. N.Y.: Dodd, Mead & Co., 1923.

Mott, Frank Luther. *A History of American Magazines. Vol. IV: 1885-1905*. Cambridge, MA: Harvard Univ. Press 1957.

Moyle, Seth. *My Friend O. Henry*. N.Y.: H.K. Fly Co., 1914.

Nye, Russel. *The Unembarrassed Muse: The Popular Arts in America*. N.Y.: The Dial Press, 1970.

O'Brien, Edward J. *The Short Story Case Book*. N.Y.: Farrar & Rinehart, Inc., 1935.

Page, Arthur W. "Little Pictures of O. Henry." *The Bookman*, 37 (June-August, 1913): 381-607.

Pattee, Fred Lewis. *The Development of the American Short Story*. N.Y.: Harper, 1923.

_____ . *The New American Literature, 1890-1930*. N.Y.: The Century Co., 1930.

Pavese, Cesare. "O. Henry; or, The Literary Trick." In Cesare Pavese. *American Literature: Essays and Opinions*. Tr. Edwin Fussell. Berkeley, CA: Univ. of Calif. Press, 1970, pp. 79-90.

Porter, William Sydney (O. Henry). *The Complete Works of O. Henry*. Fore. Harry Hansen. Garden City, N.Y.: Doubleday, 1953.

Reynolds, Quentin. *The Fiction Factory or From Pulp Row to Quality Street*. N.Y.: Random House, 1955.

Saroyan, William. "Oh What A Man Was O. Henry." *Kenyon Review*, 29 (1967): 671-75.

Sarris, Andrew. *The American Cinema*. N.Y.: E.P. Dutton, 1968.

Seldes, Gilbert. "The People and the Arts." In Bernard Rosenberg and David Manning White, eds. *Mass Culture: The Popular Arts in America*. Glencoe, Ill.: The Free Press, 1957, pp. 74-97. Rpt. from *The Great Audience*. N.Y.: Viking Press, 1950, pp. 250-84.

Simon, Paul. "Richard Cory." *Sounds of Silence.* Eclectic Music Co., Columbia Records, 1965.

Smith, C. Alphonso. *O. Henry Biography.* N.Y.: Doubleday, 1916.

Stegner, Wallace. *The Writer in America.* N.P.: Hokuseido Press, 1951.

Tracy, Paul Aubrey. *A Closer Look at O. Henry's Rolling Stone.* Master's Thesis, Univ. of Texas, 1949. In Frank Luther Mott. *A History of American Magazines. Vol. IV: 1885-1905.*

Updike, John. "The Artist and His Audience." *The New York Review of Books,* 18 July 1985, pp. 14-18.

Uzzell, Thomas H. *Narrative Technique: A Practical Course in Literary Psychology.* N.Y.: Harcourt, Brace & Co., 1923.

Van Den Haag, Ernest. "Of Happiness and of Despair We Have No Measure." In Bernard Rosenberg and David Manning White, eds. *Mass Culture: The Popular Arts in America.* Glencoe, Ill.: The Free Press, 1957, pp. 504-36.

Van Doren, Carl. "O. Henry." *Texas Review,* 2 (January 1917): 248-59.

Williams, Blanche. *A Handbook on Story Writing.* N.Y.: Dodd, Mead, & Co., 1920.

Wollen, Peter. *Signs and Meaning in The Cinema.* London: Martin Secker & Warburg, Ltd., 1969.

Woolf, Virginia. "An Essay in Criticism." In Virginia Woolf. *Granite and Rainbow.* N.Y.: Harcourt, Brace & Co., 1958, pp. 85-92. Orig. publ. in *New York Herald Tribune,* 9 October 1927.

"A Yankee Maupassant." In O. Henry. *Waifs and Strays.* Garden City, N.Y.: Doubleday, Page & Co., 1919, pp. 271-76.